Bad
Fat
Person

Gracias

I Love You

Robyn & Olina,
you are both
so beautiful!

Bad Fat Person

A Reflection on Plus-Size Bodies in a Cookie-Cutter Culture

Ali Owens

BOUNDLESS Media

ISBN: 978-1-7335512-0-5 (Paperback)
ISBN: 978-1-7335512-1-2 (eBook)

Library of Congress Control Number: 2018915191

Published by:

Boundless Media
PO Box 273178
Fort Collins, CO 80527

Printed in the United States of America

Cover photo and design by Ali Owens

For those of you who have never believed you are ~~thin beautiful attractive sexy lovable worthy~~ enough.

Contents

Author's Note

There are certain things that you just *know*.

At the age of five, I had already decided that someday, I would write books. Not just any books, mind you - *chapter* books. Lofty were my goals.

I never forgot that dream. I did, however, place it on the shelf for quite a long time - nearly thirty years, if you want the truth. Writing books remained in the realm of "someday," along with other admirable but easily delayed goals like "organize my house," "learn how to make hollandaise," and "get my shit together." There it lingered, watching the decades pass, feeling alone and neglected and wondering if I was ever going to take it down, dust it off, and let it come into being.

And finally, I did.

It wasn't so much that I made the decision to write a book as the decision tracked me down, hit me over the head, and demanded my attention. I had just been booked for a speaking engagement at a conference in Seattle, where I was to discuss body image and self-love, and like a bolt from the blue, it hit me: *I need to write a book about this.*

Instantly, I got that warm, fluttery feeling in my gut - the way you do when you know you've just come up with The Next Great Idea. Imposter syndrome, however, reared its ugly head, as it's done consistently throughout my life. It told me I would never actually finish, and that even if I did, no one would want to hear what I had to say, anyway. It demanded to know my credentials for undertaking such a task and insisted that I didn't have enough knowledge or experience to do so. It told me I was a fraud: how did I expect to help other people with their body image when I still struggled with my own?

It was a fearsome battle, and one that may have taken this dream down with it, if not for the love, support, and encouragement I received from a handful of utterly amazing human beings. These individuals patiently listened to many hours worth of emotional angst over this book. They soothed me, cajoled me, boosted my confidence, made me meditate, and reminded me to feed, wash, and clothe myself during the writing process. Together, they played a major part in drowning out the voice of self-doubt and helping this book come into being, by believing in me even when I wasn't sure I believed in myself.

To Paul McIntosh, Ryann Gaspara, Kate Farmer, Victoria Benjamin, and Audrey Owens: I could not have done this without you. Thank you for your love (of the gentle as well as tough varieties), your tireless support, and your constant affirmations of my strength, capability, wisdom, and knowledge. You are the shining stars that helped me navigate through many a long and sleepless night, and I love you all so much more than words can express.

Additionally, I owe a huge THANK YOU to everyone who contributed to my crowdfunding campaign in order to help this book come to life. The following individuals went above and beyond in their generosity:

Joann & Bill Cottrell
Charlotte Franklin
Lauren Hood
Kim Jones
Jan & Tom McIntosh
Audrey Owens
Stephanie Piltingsrud

I don't claim to have all the answers, nor have I reached a state of self-love nirvana. I still occasionally catch myself engaging in negative self-talk, bemoaning my reflection in the mirror, and comparing my body to others. Overcoming body hatred involves deprogramming ourselves of the messages we've been learning since childhood, which is an arduous process that cannot happen overnight.

However, since I began my self-love journey several years ago, I have experienced an abundance of happiness, confidence, and joy. I have accomplished things I'd previously told myself needed to wait until my body looked a certain way. I have surrounded myself with people who are truly supportive of me and my goals, instead of people who make me feel like shit. I have basically raised the bar in every single area of my life, greatly exceeding my expectations for this journey and how it would affect me.

I set out on this path with a singular goal: stop spending so much time and energy hating my body. What I found instead was so much more than a lack of hatred; it was *love*. Pure, genuine love for myself that has allowed me to create a happier and more fulfilling life than I ever dared hope for.

This is what I wish for you, too.

When we love ourselves…life, and everything in it, gets so much better.

Ali Owens
December 31st, 2018
Fort Collins, Colorado

- 1 -

Hello, I Am Fat

At the time of this writing, I am a fat person. I am a person who is, quite often, the largest one in the room. Who has to shop at specialty clothing stores. Who once came alarmingly close to getting stuck inside a go-kart. (And who, incidentally, never drove a go-kart again.)

I am the person no one wants to sit next to on the airplane. (You can practically see the *oh shit* written on their faces as they approach their row and realize I'm in it.) I'm the person others will stare at judgmentally if I so much as glance in the general direction of a Burger King. I'm the person those people assume is miserable and alone.

A man approached me once, as I sat at a restaurant enjoying lunch by myself, and gave a loud, unapologetic voice to these assumptions. "It's obvious there's no man in *your* life," he guffawed, as though he'd just made a cute joke. As though I should be starry-eyed on account of his charm. "I'm Gary - what's your name?" He extended his hand for me to shake. I just stared at it, appalled.

I'm no idiot - I'm sure he wasn't the first person to size me up and presume to know about my love life. But this *was* the first time anyone ever directly gave voice to those thoughts, and though I summoned my bravado and delivered some well-deserved pithy remark in return, there was a part of me that felt deeply, utterly ashamed. As though I'd brought this on myself. As though I should expect no less, because this is the price I should have to pay for existing in the world as a fat person.

For the record, Gary's assumption about my love life - or lack thereof - was incorrect. Not that it really matters - presuming to know someone's relationship status based on the way they look is a shitty thing to do, no matter how you slice it. Nevertheless, some people seem shocked to learn that there is someone in my life who can stand the sight of me - who can enjoy it, even.

Sometimes I am shocked, too.

I am writing this book because of that shock. Because it shouldn't be so unbelievable that I, inside this fat body, am worthy of love.

A study[1] conducted in 2015 revealed that 80% of ten-year-old girls have been on diets. And that's not all; troubling as well is the finding that more than half of girls *ages six to eight* express a desire to be thinner. These are *children*, who by all rights should be running around without a care in the world, building castles in the sand and finding shapes in the clouds -

but more and more of them are worrying about the shapes of their bodies, instead. Kids are dieting at younger and younger ages, already sold on the lie that their value is intrinsically tied to their physical appearance - a lie that so many of us, unfortunately, never call into question.

This, I believe, is unacceptable.

As a society, we are failing our younger generations, just as we ourselves were failed. We're eating what we're fed - blindly buying in to the myths about beauty, fatness, and health that have been widely accepted as truth for generations. We're perpetuating an endless cycle of shame, self-loathing, and struggle - and it's about time we stopped.

It's about time we *break* the cycle.

It's about time we teach our kids - and ourselves! - that human worth has literally nothing to do with the number on the scale.

It's about time we taught confidence instead of calorie counting. Purpose instead of pound-shedding. Self-love instead of self-deprecation.

If we could do this - if we could take all the energy we spend hating, fearing, comparing and judging and instead put it into loving ourselves just the way we are, with no strings attached…just think of how much more happiness, joy, fun, authenticity, passion, adventure, and meaning we could welcome into our lives!

So let's break down some walls, shall we?

- 2 -

Good Fat People & Bad Fat People

I have come to realize that there are two types of fat people in this world, and that they can be classified as follows.

First, there are the fat people who adhere to society's belief that their fatness renders them unworthy and unacceptable. They have been taught that their bodies are a problem, and they've bought into the sham, fallen for it hook, line, and sinker.

These people are filled with a bottomless well of shame where their bodies are concerned, and they have spent years, or perhaps even their whole lives, actively trying to take up less space in the world. Some of them go on restrictive diets and lose weight much too quickly, only to put it right back on again once they return to their normal eating habits. If they do manage to keep the extra pounds off, they live in fear of gaining them back. Many of these people ascribe a moral weight to food; they eat "good" foods like salads in public, then binge on "bad" foods at home, where no one can witness their shame. Quite a few of them have memorized the calorie counts of everything from pretzels to pumpkin seeds to Great Aunt Petunia's famous salisbury steak.

They have toxic relationships with their scales - on-again, off-again, multiple times throughout the day. Virtually all of them are saddled with the pervasive belief that their lives would somehow be magically better - problems solved, social skills sharpened, success level elevated - if only they could lose weight. These are the Good Fat People: adequately shamed into submission and fully brainwashed into believing they are defined by their bodies.

This isn't our fault - it's how our culture trains us to be. From a young age, we are prepped, groomed, and prepared to accept our punishment, should we ever expand beyond an appropriate dress size. The way society writes the story, it's only okay to be fat if you're either A) hating yourself for being fat, or B) actively trying *not* to be fat.

And then, there are the misfits. The rebels. The type of fat people that society loves to hate. The ones who don't give a flying fuck what anyone else thinks. These are the people who embrace every curve; who wear horizontal stripes and short shorts in a blatant display of fuck-the-man confidence, figurative middle fingers jabbed skyward. These people will order a cheeseburger and a milkshake if that's what they want, regardless of the fact that others may judge them for not opting for something twelve-thousand-percent fat-free. The rule-breakers, the ass-shakers, the black sheep - the Bad Fat People.

Society likes to look down on these people. We write them off as ignorant, uneducated, or downright stupid: they'd *have* to be, in order to be so blithely unaware of the vast discrepancy between how our culture has told us we should look and how they *actually* look, right? This assumption, of course, is rooted in a tragic unawareness that some fat people actually *don't* loathe their bodies.

Why? Why do we hate fat and fat people so much? Why do we encourage and cheer for a fat person on a weight-loss journey, but mock, shame, and discriminate against fat folks who don't feel the need to change? This dichotomy is indicative of a deep-seated (and mostly misinformed) prejudice that thrives in our culture today, despite the push in more recent years for equality and acceptance of all people across various races, ethnicities, genders, gender identities, sexualities, abilities, and religious beliefs. Many of us now understand that discriminating against people for these reasons is wrong, but while some folks, especially those who align themselves with the ideals of modern feminism, recognize body shaming as yet another unacceptable form of discrimination, many others, sadly, do not.

For most of my time as a fat person, I have been a Good Fat Person. I have loathed myself, shamed myself, and not blamed anyone else for shaming me, either. I have accepted the belief that I am inadequate because of the amount of space I take up in the world, and I have poured a lot of time, money and energy into reducing that space. I believed that, as a fat person, I had no right to ever *not* be on a diet. I had no right to be accepting of my body as it was.

As I embarked on my self-love journey, which I will detail throughout this book, the landscape of these ingrained beliefs shifted, and slowly but surely, I came to acknowledge and respect not just my fat body, but also the fact that being fat *wasn't a terrible thing to be*, nor was it a defining feature of my personality, attitude, ambition, or intelligence.

I slowly began posting photos of myself on social media that I would have gone to great lengths to keep hidden before - photos in which my hefty upper arms and plump, round face were clearly visible. I'd begun realizing that I didn't have to apologize for my body. I wrote articles about body image and published them online, professing my acceptance of what had previously seemed unacceptable. In a sense, it felt like I was "coming out" as a fat person. I'd tried for so long to hide it.

It's funny, really, because all it takes is a glance in my direction to see that I carry a lot more fat on my body than the average person. No amount of shapewear, empire waists, or big, flowing caftans (you know, the kind meant to "flatter" plus size folks but that hang like the tragically fashion-forward equivalent of a shower curtain) will hide this fact. I *knew* this - but my shame over my fat body was so deeply ingrained that I felt I needed to do whatever I could to hide my bulk *anyway*, out of respect for the poor, tender retinas of those who happened to look my way.

When I stopped hiding, the freedom was exhilarating and terrifying, simultaneously.

Suddenly, I'd given myself permission to talk about the elephant in the room - my fatness - without following it with a hasty qualifier: "...but I'm starting on this awesome new diet tomorrow, and I'm going to lose it all!" It didn't *need* a qualifier anymore; it was just who I was. And it was... *fine*.

For the first time in my life as a fat person, I wasn't trying to lose weight. Instead, I was putting my time and energy toward living my life. I was connecting with people on a deeper level. I was starting a business. I was traveling. I was learning new things. I was wearing swimsuits on the beach in Mexico, not caring how "offended" all the regular-sized people would be and instead just enjoying the hell out of myself, haters be damned. I was writing, I was creating, I was advocating for body positivity and personal empowerment - and it was the truest, most authentic expression of myself. I was fat, and I was happy - two things I'd never previously believed could simultaneously exist. In short, I was being a Bad Fat Person - and it came with a sense of freedom that I'd never truly experienced until then.

In May of 2017, I accompanied my dear friend Kate on a vacation to Amsterdam - a trip that ended up being quite arguably among the happiest ten days of my life. Though I was generally always the largest person in the vicinity wherever I went, I could barely bring myself to notice; I was too busy drinking in the sights, sounds, smells, and intoxicating *otherness* that always lights me up when I travel, especially internationally.

On our second afternoon in that impossibly beautiful city, we were taking a stroll through Serphatipark, in the lovely Bohemian arts district of De Pijp, when I tripped over a loose stone and fell to my knees. This was nothing out of the ordinary, really; I've never been graceful. In fact, at the time of this writing, I *still* have twin bruises on each of my shins from the time I fell *up* (yes, up) a flight of concrete steps over three years ago. (My doctor has assured me that, though harmless, the pigment is essentially tattooed onto my body at this point and will probably never disappear completely.) In certain circles, I'm kind of known for being The Lady That Falls Down A Lot. What can I say? It's true.

In Amsterdam, however, though my fall was minor, my lower extremities were still a bit swollen from eleven hours of air travel, and possibly because of this, my leg bruised like a rotting banana: *all over*. The whole thing was black and purple, and so inflamed I couldn't even bend my knee. I didn't let that stop me, however - I was in the Netherlands, dammit, and travel is one of my favorite things in the world, and I flat-out *refused* to spend my vacation watching Netflix with my leg propped up on the couch, thank you very much. So I went about my daily activities, ignoring the pain and having an overall incredible time, my balloon-sized knee notwithstanding.

When Kate and I returned stateside, I promptly scheduled a doctor's appointment, just to ensure I hadn't done any long-term damage to my knee. The great news was that I hadn't - it was very badly bruised, but unbroken in every sense of the word. However, a new problem cropped up - a blood clot, the result of taking an eleven-hour flight home with all that blood pooling around in my leg. I hadn't even thought about that. In retrospect, I was very lucky; things could have been so much worse. All because of a run-of-the-mill fall in the park.

As my knee healed, I found myself coming to terms with the fact that, despite my newfound acceptance of my body, it wasn't very strong. My sense of balance was shit - I'd known this even as a thin person. What if, I mused, I could do something to build my strength so that I could hopefully avoid situations like this in the future?

That was a scary thing to contemplate, in all honesty. I belonged to a gym, but the last time I'd gone, a muscular hulk of a man had stared, open-mouthed, as I worked out my quads on the leg press. I'd immediately felt hideous and gargantuan, and I hadn't gone back after that.

Additionally, I had to wonder how my toxic relationship with the scale would play out, should I begin a regular exercise regimen. I had made *so* much headway in the last couple years toward loving my fat body, and I was terrified that if I started working out - something so many people do with the express purpose of losing weight - I'd revert back to my old patterns. I didn't want to revisit the seemingly endless cycle of shaming myself, starving myself, and hating myself.

Besides, if I was trying to lose weight, how could I call myself a body-positive activist? Wasn't I writing a bunch of stuff about how we shouldn't *have* to lose weight in order to love ourselves? I worried that if I got smaller, my audience would see me as a hypocrite. You guys, this shit is *complicated.* A whole cocktail of confusing emotions was surfacing, and it was nearly paralyzing.

Tentatively, I wondered if it would be possible to work with a trainer who understood where I was coming from - who could help me focus on feeling strong and energetic and badass, *not* on losing weight. I made an appointment with a local trainer who was recommended to me by a friend, unsure of what to expect.

To my delight, this woman *completely* got it. Once I'd explained to her a bit about my lifelong struggle for body acceptance, she assured me that we could tailor a training program to zero in on how I *felt*, not how I looked. We decided that I wouldn't weigh in - I'd broken up with my scale years before and didn't really want to jump back into *that* toxic relationship again. Instead, I would just move my body in ways that would get my blood flowing and make my muscles stronger.

So I did what had previously seemed fairly impossible.

I started working out.

I met my trainer at the gym three times a week, where she'd walk me through all manner of exercises I hadn't known my body was capable of carrying out. She said my form was beautiful and told me I was a natural dead-lifter. To my surprise, I found that I wasn't hating our workouts. I won't say I *enjoyed* them - I've never been one of those types who finds great pleasure in exercise - but they didn't feel like torture, either, which was something new.

Still, I was hyper-aware that I was almost always the largest person there. Occasionally, other trainers would be working with their clients nearby, and I'd wonder what they thought about my gut hanging over my waistband, or my fat ass in my stretchy pants. *At least they all know I'm working out*, I placated myself one day while completing a set of squats. *I may be fat, but at least they know I'm being a GOOD fat person.*

The thought nearly stopped me in my tracks. I was doing the very thing I write about *not* doing: I was ascribing a moral weight to fatness and health. I was insinuating to myself that I was worth more as a person because I was going to the gym - because I'd become ever-so-slightly smaller and tighter as a byproduct of moving around a lot more. *I was taking comfort in the fact that they were seeing me working out and most likely assuming I was there to lose weight - to not be fat anymore.* In their eyes, I felt, that made me a better person - more acceptable, more worthy.

I caught the thought and squashed it down like a mosquito in Zika season, but I found the dichotomy between *good* fat people and *bad* fat people interesting enough that I kept ruminating on it in the weeks that followed. Eventually, I ruminated on it *so much* that a title was born, followed by a lot of words that came together to form this book.

≷

The truth is, most fat people live their lives on the Good list. It seems easier - put your head down, don't rock the boat, do what you're told.

Additionally, some people who aren't even fat have made a commitment, consciously or otherwise, to live by the rules of the Good list. Perhaps these people carry a little extra weight. Perhaps they've weight-cycled their entire lives, going from fat to thin and back again. Or perhaps the perceived flaws in their bodies are visible to them alone. You do not need to be obese to fat-shame yourself - and to internalize the fat-shaming that happens on the regular in our thin-obsessed society.

But how often do we really consider everything that goes into living as a Good Fat Person? How often do we really ponder the soul-crushing-ness of it all? In order to quantify it - and because I can be a snarky little shit - I have created a list of handy guidelines. Read on.

HOW TO BE A GOOD FAT PERSON

1. Eat nothing but salads - and leave the dressing on the side, damn it!
2. If you must binge, do so in the seclusion of your own home, with the curtains drawn. And please be kind enough to wear sweatpants and a ratty t-shirt while you're doing it, and make sure Dorito crumbs end up all over your chest so society can maintain its vision

of fat folk as sloppy and slovenly, thank you very much.

3. Berate your own appearance constantly. Make sure everyone - friends, family, coworkers, your Lyft driver, and the guy on the phone who helped you troubleshoot your internet connection last week - knows just how much you hate yourself due to your size. Otherwise, you may give the impression that you are perfectly fine with the way you look (which, of course, is strictly prohibited).

4. Always, always, *always* be actively striving to make yourself smaller - because as you know, the only way to be an acceptable fat person is *to be trying not to be a fat person.*

5. Work out, damn it, because all of us are worried about your health - but could you do it at home, so we don't have to see your big ass in those yoga pants?

6. Always take the stairs instead of the elevator, and always pass up the front-row parking spot in favor of one about twelve miles away. The walk will be good for you.

7. Single? Don't even try to date - you're offending the rest of the people on OkCupid. In a relationship? Don't rock the boat! Beggars can't be choosers, and you're *lucky* someone is willing to put up with you and your body. Avoid saying or doing anything that could be construed as criticism toward your partner - otherwise, they'll leave you and you'll die alone.

8. Never, under any circumstances, so much as *hint* at the fact that you are a sexual being. This will only disgust all the nice, normal people who will be forced to imagine having sex with your fat body.

9. Be sure to develop a boisterous and self-deprecating sense of humor so that you have something to offer all the regular-sized people who so generously donate their friendship to you.

10. Try not to be too ambitious or successful - you'll only confuse people, as everyone knows fat folks are naturally lazy and unmotivated.

11. Understand that careers involving a prominent place in the public eye are out of your reach, and adhere to this unquestioningly. Following your dreams is overrated, after all, and no one likes a fatty in the spotlight!

12. Ladies, be sure to follow the dress code issued by society upon those of you with excess bulk. (See accompanying literature below.)

DRESS CODE FOR FAT WOMEN & FEMMES

The first and most important thing to adhere to is a firm commitment never to wear any garments from the following list of banned clothing items:

- Yoga pants
- Leggings

- Anything that shows your knees
- Anything form-fitting enough to display your actual form
- Lingerie (being seen buying this in public will give the impression that you're an actual human being with a sex drive, and as we all know, fat people are too gross to have those)
- Horizontal stripes (they'll make you look wider)
- Strappy shoes (they're essentially a pair of Play-Doh Fun Factories for your feet)
- Crop tops
- Short shorts
- Regular-length shorts
- Tank tops (you mustn't let those upper arms show)
- Swimwear of any kind
- Designer clothing (fortunately, you'll rarely encounter this hurdle, as *very* few prominent designers even make their garments in your size, conveniently saving you the hassle of thinking for a moment you could actually pull off *haute couture*)
- Anything with cutouts
- A short haircut (admittedly, this is not *clothing*, per se, but everyone knows short cuts aren't flattering for round faces. Society much prefers double chins to be shrouded in a curtain of hair, thank you very much).
- Anything made of pleather or vinyl (too shiny - you'll call attention to yourself)
- Anything with sequins or excessive adornments (too sparkly - you'll call attention to yourself)

- Anything with a large pattern (too loud - you'll call attention to yourself)
- Anything with bright colors (too bold - you'll call attention to yourself)

Certainly there are more garments available to the general public that fat women and femmes should not wear under any circumstances, but frankly, I've run out of space to list them all. Above all else, remember that your body is *not* a thing of beauty to be appreciated, but rather a malady that should cause you great shame.

The general rule of thumb? *When in doubt, cover that shit.* (And when you're not in doubt, cover it anyway, because your body makes people uncomfortable.)

Do you find this list to be too restrictive? Worry not, my fellow fatty - plenty of fashion options exist that will cater to your size! For example, we urge you to wear all the corsets and otherwise restrictive shapewear your bank account will allow you to possess! Breathing, after all, is overrated. And have you forgotten the ever-versatile Long Flowing Dress? They're quite lovely - even more so if they're of the high-necked and long-sleeved variety. In the absence of available LFDs, you can make one yourself by cutting a hole in the center of a large blanket and sticking your head through it. Voila - you've successfully hidden your shame!

Just remember, ladies: all it takes is strict adherence to this list, and you're well on your way to being a Good Fat

Person! Our brainwashed society thanks you for your compliance.

⋙

I may sound flippant, but underneath this veneer of sarcasm and derision, my heart aches. The sheer amount of effort it takes to stay on the Good list, day in and day out, is staggering - yet so many of us choose this over the alternative.

What exactly *is* the alternative?

Acceptance? Not quite. It's too passive a word, devoid of intensity and powerless to indicate the magnitude of the journey.

Some would say that if we're not on the Good list, we're *giving up* or *letting ourselves go*. But that's not it, either.

Resignation? On the contrary.

The alternative to living our lives by the rules of the Good list is...

Unconditional self love.

Yes - *even if we're fat.*

If we can learn to love ourselves, with no strings attached, *just as we are*...we render the rules obsolete.

You see, when we live by the Good list, we can pat ourselves on the back all we want for following the rules... but what we fail to even examine is the fact that *the very system that's generating those rules* is intrinsically, irretrievably flawed.

After all, if the system is broken, it's pretty safe to say the rules that uphold it are, as well.

Yet we fail to question. To look beyond the veil to the heart of the problem. Spoiler alert: *the problem isn't your body.*

Just *look* at all the rules and limitations we've created for ourselves around cultural notions of beauty. Even as a skinny person, I very rarely wore shorts, due to a lifelong belief that I didn't have "good legs." What I wanted were long, smooth, exquisite gams that tapered off into dainty little feet. What I had were thighs that rubbed against each other no matter how much weight I lost, cellulite, flat doughy knees, wide calves, and - the bane of my existence - cankles. Oh, how I loathed the lower halves of my legs, which, to my self-scrutinizing eyes, looked like bed pillows stuffed into shoes. I saw a photo once of my great grandmother sitting in a chair, cankles on full display beneath the modest hem of her dress, and I seethed at her, even though she'd died many years before, for muddying the family gene pool with those tree trunks she called legs.

So I developed a rule for myself. Since wearing heels gave my seemingly nonexistent ankles an ever-so-slight bit of definition, I only allowed myself to wear clothing that displayed my legs if it was paired with a set of heels at least a couple inches high. This meant, of course, that if I was doing anything active or outdoorsy, I had to wear pants, as hiking in heels didn't end up being a great idea. (Yes, I've tried it; yes, it's a good way to break your ankle.)

That wasn't the only rule I set for myself, of course. I never wore form-fitting shirts if I felt the least bit bloated. I could only ever wear that blouse that tended to ride up a little in the back with a very specific pair of jeans that covered up the love handles I was convinced I had. And any kind of leggings or stretchy pants absolutely *had* to be paired with an oversize sweater or t-shirt, long enough to cover my rear end (which was, in my mind, grotesque, distorted, and big enough to be seen from space).

Note, too, that these were the rules I'd put in place for myself when I was *thin*. You don't even want to know how many would get added to the pot whenever I started to gain weight.

The funny thing about these rules is that I don't think many of us actively *decide* on them. We just register our reflections, feel all sorts of shame about a certain part or six of our bodies, and submit to that shame. I know I never made the conscious decision to hike in heels - "Hey, this will be fun!" - it's just that I didn't see any other options.

Also funny is how stringently so many of us follow these unspoken rules we set for ourselves. Looking back, follow-through hasn't always been my strong suit. I've spent a lot of my life making resolutions, setting goals, and laying out plans, only to turn my back on them as soon as the going got rough. But my rules about the ways in which it was acceptable to present my body to the world? They were *unwavering*. They were set in stone, frozen in time, and written into the stars - or at least, you'd have thought so, based on the fervor with which I obeyed them. If I had, say, invested money with the same kind of single-minded dedication, I'd be a millionaire many times over by now.

When it comes down to it, the rules were one of the most important things in my life. They were a driving factor in everything I did. They occupied a ridiculous amount of my time and energy. I spent *so* many years of my life tottering around in painful heels, sweating under big, baggy clothes in the hot summers, and just generally sacrificing physical comfort *because I believed my appearance alone didn't warrant such a right.*

This is why I've written this book. *This* is why I feel such a need to address our culture's fucked-up beauty standards: because we follow them at all costs, to the point of obsession, and often to the detriment of our own well-being. Why? Because we're told that achieving physical "success" - that is, possessing a societally acceptable body - will bring us...*happiness.*

The same happiness we sacrifice by following all these strict rules and trying to attain the unattainable.

It's ironic. It's really, *really* sad.

What if we could just be happy with ourselves, *as we are?* If that seems like a foreign concept, you're not alone; plenty of people share your skepticism, and I used to be one of them. I didn't believe it was possible for me to be happy - truly happy - unless I looked a certain way, wore a certain size, and weighed in at a certain number. I've heard many, many other people, particularly women, express a similar belief.

Are we really buying into the lie that our happiness is contingent on our physical appearance? That the way we look matters so much that it can actually act as the *sole inhibitor of our own bliss?*

We are. And it's got to stop, for everyone's sake.

The answer - the antidote - is unconditional self love.

Talking about loving oneself is the easy part. Overhauling our emotional landscape in order to achieve it is something else entirely. We'll get to that, later on - but first, let me leave you with this seed.

No matter how you slice it, being a Good Fat Person requires a lot of sacrifice. It requires us to relinquish certain freedoms - freedoms no one ever asks thin people to hand over - and replace them with a whole plethora of restrictions about what we can eat, what we can wear, and even how much we are allowed to *like* ourselves. It requires us to put really important things on hold - things like applying for a better job or taking a well-deserved vacation or even appearing in family photos - for an arbitrary future moment in which we will have "fixed" ourselves. It requires us to believe we have no business feeling good about ourselves unless we can starve, exercise, and shrink our bodies enough to fit into societal norms.

Do you really want to live *that* way?

Or would you rather just *live?*

- 3 -

The F-Word

First, there's something we need to discuss, and that is the dreaded F-word. No, not the one you think (although, as you'll realize, I'm quite fond of that one as well). I'm talking about the word that strikes fear into the hearts of many - the word that has us clutching our proverbial pearls in horror due to the extreme *awfulness* of it all.

Fat.

Fat, fat, fat.

There. I've said it. In fact, I say it all the time - as you've no doubt noticed by now - and in all honesty, I've grown to appreciate it.

It hasn't always been this way, though. For most of my life, my relationship with the word *fat* was quite toxic indeed. I looked at it the way most people do: as a horrible insult, a terrible thing to be. Throughout my life, from my adolescence on up, I've had a countless number of conversations such as this:

Friend: I look so fat in these jeans.

Me: You're not fat! You're beautiful!

What's wrong with this picture?

Unfortunately, I was eschewing the flawed yet widely-held and societally accepted belief that *fat* and *beautiful* lived at entirely opposite ends of the same spectrum - as though the two were mutually exclusive, incapable of existing in tandem with one another. And I believed that - of *course* I did. Having bought into the rampant beauty standards we've all been spoon-fed by our thin-obsessed culture practically from birth, the notion that anyone could be fat *and* beautiful was laughable. Fat was a disqualifier - *everyone* knew that.

Because of our messed-up notions of fat and what it insinuates, here's another example of a conversation that I've had (a lot) more than once:

Me *(not in a self-deprecating tone, simply stating facts)*: These chairs were not built with fat people in mind.

Other Person: You're not fat, you're beautiful!

Me: Well, thank you! I'm also fat.

Other Person *(visibly distressed)*: Don't *say* that about yourself!

Me: But why not? I *am* fat. It's okay to say it.

Other Person: You're *not* fat!

Me: ....

I mean, have they *seen* me? I always wonder what people are trying to accomplish with conversations like these.

Do they think their flat-out denial of my size will somehow erase my awareness of my round belly and thick thighs? Do they assume that my willingness to use the word *fat* to describe myself comes from a deep-seated place of self-hatred and insecurity, despite my insistence to the contrary?

Whatever the reason, conversations like these illustrate a commonly held but entirely flawed belief system that FAT = BAD.

This is precisely why I've chosen to reclaim the F-word - and I've found tremendous power in doing so.

JUST SO WE'RE CLEAR...

What *is* fat? Without getting too scientific about the whole thing, fat is simply an oily substance, naturally occurring in animal bodies, that's generally deposited as a layer beneath the skin. Some of us have very little of it. Others of us have more of it. Still others of us have a *lot* of it. It is but one deviation in the vast range of real live human bodies. There are others, of course. Some people have green eyes. Narrow feet. Freckles. The variations of the human form are myriad, and for the most part, we seem to understand and accept this...until fat enters the equation.

We don't ascribe a certain moral weight to things like eye color, feet, or freckles...so why do we do it with fat?

Frankly, it's about damn time we stopped.

I have been many things in my life, including very thin and very fat. My adult weight has vacillated back and forth between 116 pounds at my lightest and well over 250 pounds at my heaviest. With these drastic fluctuations in my body has come a *lot* of confusion about the ways in which I identify inside it.

Regardless of how my body shrank or grew over the years, I never felt comfortable within it. "I'm a thin person trapped in a large body," I would remark during my college years, after quickly gaining quite a lot of weight (the Freshman 15, for me, was more like the Freshman 75). But later on, in my early twenties, I lost over a hundred pounds, and even though everyone around me was telling me I was skinny, and my clothing size went from a 22 to a two…I felt like an imposter, a fraud. Despite my earlier insistence that I was thin at heart, once I actually *got* thin, I felt, conversely, like a fat girl masquerading as a skinny person. Despite my much smaller size, I didn't feel any better about myself. I just felt like a big, fat fake.

This meant that *no matter my size, I never felt legitimate.* I was never a *real* fat person or a *real* thin person. It didn't matter how much I weighed - I'd see myself in photographs taken just the day before and not even recognize myself, so utterly disconnected was I with my physical being. My mind and body were so out of sync that I didn't even know what I looked like - *really* looked like - at all. I was never grounded in my body. Instead, I felt like I was living just outside it, a shapeless form, connected to nothing at all.

It wasn't until my early thirties, having re-gained the hundred pounds and another fifty to boot, when I began to realize that this disconnect wasn't born out of mere indifference, but out of a deep *hatred* for my body. It dawned on me that no matter how small I'd gotten over the years, it had never been good enough; I'd *still* felt a distressing, obsessive need to shrink even more - to take up less and less space. I had developed a bitter resentment for my physical form, one that began with the onset of puberty, and to escape the uncomfortable feelings, I disassociated. My hatred of my own body was preventing me from really living inside it.

When I realized this, I knew something had to change. I was tired of hating myself, tired of loathing the body I was born with, tired of comparing myself to others and always coming up lacking. I noticed that every time I looked in the mirror, it was to observe how beautiful I would be *if I wasn't fat*. I could see beauty within myself - but it always came with the massive condition of losing half of my body weight! When I would scan the shape of my body in the mirror, I would perform mental edits as I went, imagining a slimming of the waist here, a flattening of the stomach there, a toning of the upper arms and thighs, and the removal of the vast majority of my ass. And I realized that, up until that point, I'd never actually taken in my reflection *just as it was*. I didn't honestly know what I even looked like without all those mental filters.

To counteract this, I began looking at my reflection in the mirror - *really* looking. I stripped naked and let my eyes wander over my belly, my breasts, my thighs, my butt. I took in my lumps and bumps, my stretch marks, my cellulite, and paid attention to the thoughts that came. *Fat. Disgusting. Sickening. Tub of lard. Vomit-inducing. Ugly. Unlovable. Unworthy.*

I wasn't prepared for the wave of shame and self-hatred that crashed over me as I looked myself in the eyes and let these words float around in my head. I felt physically sick; my eyes brimmed over with tears. *No wonder I dissociate from my body,* I thought to myself. *These thoughts are far too painful to endure.*

My immediate urge was to punish myself: lock myself in my third-floor apartment, throw all my food out the window, and not allow myself to emerge until I'd starved away into a regular-sized person. (I'm no stranger to self-harm, and for me, it's always taken the form of food, be it too much or too little.) Instead, I fought that instinct and turned my criticism not toward myself, but toward the *words* I was using. *Fat. Disgusting. Sickening. Tub of lard. Vomit-inducing. Ugly. Unlovable. Unworthy.*

Again, the shame nearly slapped me across the face, but I stood firm against it, the way we do when we brace ourselves against a strong wind. I kept repeating this ritual, day in and day out, and when the hateful words came flying at me, I'd visualize myself deflecting them, Space Invaders style.

Ugly.

Pew-pew!

Sickening.

Blam!

Unworthy.

Kapow!

The one I couldn't seem to shake, however, was *fat*. I simply couldn't deny that it was true. The others could be argued. I mean, maybe I wasn't really vomit-inducing, since no one had actually vomited at the sight of me (to my knowledge, anyway). And I knew, logically, that I wasn't unlovable, due to the people in my life who consistently purported to love me. But fat? I couldn't reason my way out of that one. It wasn't dysmorphia; it was *fact*.

Slowly, the realization dawned on me: if I wanted the self-hatred to go away - and oh, how I did - somehow, some way, I was going to have to make peace with my fat. I was going to have to alter my belief system so that "fat" was no longer synonymous with all those other terrible words.

I took my ritual to the next level. Every day, on my way in to the shower, I'd stand naked in front of the bathroom mirror, take in my body in all its roly-poly glory, as I had before, and say to myself, in a neutral and conversational tone, "I'm fat" - the same way I might say "I'm right-handed." Even-keeled and devoid of judgment. Easy and breezy. No big deal.

It sure *felt* like a big deal, though. I did this every day for weeks, and each time, I had to fight against the onslaught of self-flagellation. The shame churned in my stomach like vomit threatening to make an appearance; I could even taste it, acrid and bitter on my tongue. Every time, I'd swallow it down, and every time, the effort required to do so left me nearly trembling. *Not today, shame. I refuse to give you any more power over me.*

Some days were better than others. Sometimes I managed to stand my ground. But on quite a few occasions, the shame snuck past my defenses to whisper hateful things in my ear.

"I'm fat."

Unacceptable.

"I'm fat."

How dare you.

"I'm fat."

You are irretrievably fucked up and I hate you so much.

During that time I felt, quite literally, that I was at war.

One day in particular was especially cruel. I'd been feeling emboldened to call people out for their sexist bullshit and had begun to comment about these things on social media, rather than hiding my opinions for fear of causing conflict. This particular day, I'd remarked on some problematic comments following an article about rape culture, and the trolls had come a-calling, a plague of misogynist locusts bound and determined to punish me for daring to speak out against them. The hate and vitriol only intensified once they looked through my photos and learned what I looked like.

"You just wish you were hot enough to rape, you fat piece of shit."

"You're one of those ugly bitches who cry rape to make the world think people actually want to fuck you."

This was a common theme, and even though I knew I should have followed the cardinal rule of staying sane on the internet - which is, of course, *for the love of all that is holy, don't read the comments* - I couldn't stop myself. By the time I got home at the end of the day, I felt insignificant, worthless, and dangerously vulnerable.

I stormed into the bathroom to take a shower. I was *angry*. Angry with the horrible people who had said such awful things, of course - but I was also angry with *myself*. I was angry with myself for thinking I could make a difference. For thinking I actually knew something about equality. For putting myself out there when it was obvious no one would ever take me seriously - not as long as I looked the way I did.

I yanked my shirt up over my head and threw it, venomously, into a crumpled heap on the floor. Then, I kicked off my jeans with such ferocity that I nearly fell over in the process. Once I was naked, I glanced in the mirror and saw the pain and fury in my own eyes, looking back at me.

"*I'm fat!*" I shouted at my reflection in anguish. "*I'm fucking fat, okay?*"

I watched my face, saw the hate in it, noticed the shapes my mouth formed while saying those words. It made me even angrier, so I yelled back, at the top of my lungs.

"*SO FUCKING WHAT???*"

A brief moment of silence, and then...I started laughing.

Why? Because I was yelling at myself in the mirror, for crying out loud. Because, I realized, there was wisdom in what I'd just screamed. So I was fat. *So what?*

To say my self-love journey ended there would be a gross exaggeration, but the amount of headway I made by uttering those three little words - *so fucking what* - was significant.

I know all this talking-to-myself-in-the-mirror stuff may sound like a bunch of touchy-feely mumbo-jumbo to some of you, but the truth is that this was a turning point for me. Without really understanding the full extent of what I was doing, I'd reclaimed the word *fat* and turned it into something that better served me. The intensity of the word was gone - it no longer had the power to carry shame or judgment. It was simply a descriptor, much like "short" or "blond" or "tan."

The funny thing was, as soon as I owned the word, I *immediately* felt in sync with my body - as though I was at home within it, in a way I'd never been before. And simply stepping into myself like that was enough to hinder so much of the hatred I'd been flinging at myself for years.

There have been many steps in my self-love journey. It's been a long and arduous process that has taken place over a matter of years, and is still ongoing to this day. In a world that loves to hate fatness, I doubt the journey will ever really be finished. It will, most likely, be something I have to live by, consciously, every day until the end of time. But the transformation couldn't even have begun until I first acknowledged my dissociation with my body, my deep and lifelong hatred for it, and the problematic beliefs I held about fat and fatness. It seems silly to say that talking to myself in the mirror changed my life…but it's true.

All this is why I have such an unlikely affinity for the dreaded F-word. Because to me, it doesn't mean lazy, or stupid, or unlovable, or ugly. It symbolizes the freedom to really see myself as I am and release the judgment around it. It means that if a random stranger on the street were to stop me and say, "Hey, you're fat," I wouldn't break down in tears, the way I would have several years ago. Instead of beating myself up for bothering someone else with my size, I'd simply shake my head in pity and feel sorry for the poor fool whose life was so wretchedly boring that scrutinizing other people's bodies felt like a necessary thing to do.

And that, my friends, is empowerment.

FAT IS NOT A BAD WORD

It is important to note that just because I am personally comfortable with the word *fat* does not mean that every fat person wishes to be addressed as such. Everyone's got their own preference. Plus-size, curvy, voluptuous, chubby, thick - there are no shortage of words out there, and it's the prerogative of fat people to use whichever words empower us most.

That said, I am a firm believer in never, not *ever*, looking at the word "fat" as a bad word. Say it with me: FAT IS NOT A BAD WORD. Now write it down on a piece of paper and put it in your wallet and look at it twenty times a day, or maybe tattoo it on your arm. Yes, it's *that* important.

Why?

I'm glad you asked.

A friend of mine recently told me about an interaction she had with her five-year-old son, Tristan. One day, Tristan came home from kindergarten with the news that he'd had a substitute teacher in class. When his mother asked what the teacher was like, he responded, "She was fat." There was no emotion attached to this statement - he was simply telling it like it was.

His mother, however, was horrified. "Listen, Tristan," she told him. "That's not a nice word. We don't *ever* say that word, do you understand?"

Tristan nodded, then went back to his box of toys, a new correlation between fatness and badness firmly placed upon his impressionable young mind.

Weeks after this incident, my friend and I were having a conversation about body positivity and the importance of words, and she suddenly clamped her hand over her mouth, thinking of the message she'd inadvertently sent to her son. When she told me what Tristan had said and how she'd responded, it was clear that her intentions had been good: she wanted to ensure her son never turned into that bully - because there's one in every classroom - picking on other kids and calling them fat. Which I can *totally* get behind.

But the approach? Not so much.

Here's the thing: when we tell our kids that fat is a bad word, *our message carries the implication that fat, in and of itself, is bad.* By insisting that the word is negative, we unwittingly link negative feelings toward fat and fat people - because *why would fat be a bad word unless it was a terrible thing to be?* When we tiptoe around these three little letters, we are ascribing moral value to fat itself - and subsequently giving the impression that fat people are sub-par. By demonizing the word, we're demonizing the thing itself.

"But I don't mean it like *that,*" says someone, inevitably, every time I discuss this issue. And I'm sure you don't. I'm sure your intentions are nothing but golden. The reality, however, is: *impact is greater than intent.* And even though you may not *intend* to give your child, or anyone else, for that matter, a negative outlook on fat people, the *impact* is that that's *exactly what you're doing* - and it needs to stop.

Think about it. All the "replacement" words - curvy, voluptuous, full-figured, and their ilk - are used to take the edge off the dreaded F-word. They minimize it, water it down, and make it seem less than what it actually is. And the message this sends to kids and adults alike is that it's fine to be curvy or voluptuous or full-figured, but not to be actually, *really* fat - because being actually, *really* fat is such a terrible thing that you must never notice it or acknowledge it.

You guys - fat is not Voldemort. It's not this evil thing lurking away in some dark corner of the world, ready to unleash doom and destruction on all of civilization if someone so much as speaks its name. Fat isn't shameful. *It is literally something we all possess on our bodies, because we need it to survive.* Can we please stop pretending it's the worst thing we could possibly have?

By doing this - by attaching all this negativity to fat and fatness - we ensure that future generations will grow up like so many of us did: with a sense of profound inadequacy for possessing even a little bit of it, *despite the fact that possessing it is biologically necessary.* It's a recipe for self-hatred.

Is that what you want for your children?

Probably not.

≳

One more thing.

I am also a firm believer in never, *not ever*, making unsolicited comments about other people's bodies.

Period.

But what if it's a nice comment??? I hear you asking. Surely you can't mean....???

Oh, but I do.

I have a friend named Anna who is classically and conventionally beautiful. Thin, lithe, feminine features, bright eyes, big smile - the works. Not long ago, she confided in me that, though she doesn't have many issues with her body image, it upsets her that her aunt, who she's very close with, comments on her body every time they get together.

"It's always one of the first things she says - that I look really thin in that dress or I look like I've lost weight. She says it as a compliment - and it's funny, because you'd think having someone tell you that you look thinner would be a good thing, but honestly it just makes me feel uncomfortable. Like, *why* are you paying so much attention to my body? Why are you keeping track? It's just weird."

Anna has a point, and I've noticed this phenomenon with people in my own life. Fairly regularly, someone will comment that I look like I've lost weight - which is especially odd when I happen to *know* I haven't lost an ounce. And it seems like every damn day, I hear at least one person making observations about someone else's body. "So-and-so looks like she's dropped a few pounds," an acquaintance will remark, leaving me to wonder, for the trillion-and-eleventh time, *why* we, as humans, are so damn obsessed with each other's measurements.

Why do people observe my fat body and feel the need to tell me that it looks smaller? Most of the time, we both know damn well it's not true - and even if it was, why talk about it at all? Are we really *that* desperate for something to discuss? Is there really *nothing else* to say? What if, instead of commenting on bodies at all, we talked about something of substance? What if we complimented our friends, acquaintances, colleagues, classmates and family members on their intelligence? Their sharp wit? Their sparkling personality? It's these things, after all, that make us who we are. We're the *driver,* not the vehicle. Let's talk about that, instead.

Full disclosure: I'm just as guilty as the next person. I realized a couple of years ago that when interacting with female children and toddlers, my inclination was always to tell them how pretty they looked. I was always commenting on some aspect of their appearance: "Your hair looks beautiful today" or "You're so pretty in that dress." At the time, I thought nothing of it. It wasn't until recently that I realized the lesson these girls absorb through those comments, the way I absorbed the lessons of my own: *everyone, everywhere, is paying attention to how you look.*

I was a pretty child, in a conventional sense, and people told me so. I was praised for it, as though it was something I'd achieved. And the takeaway that I carried into adolescence, then adulthood, was that *being pretty matters.* People *like* you if you're pretty. If you're pretty, it's one of the most important things about you. People are always paying attention to how pretty you are.

It's a message I could have done without.

Let's circle back to Tristan and his mother's unintentionally ineffective response to his description of his substitute teacher as fat. What could his mother have said instead?

How about, "Okay, that's what she *looked* like, and it's really cool that there are so many ways for people to look, but looks don't really tell us much about who someone is, so we shouldn't focus on that. What else did you notice about her? Was she kind? Funny? Did she help you learn anything?"

This kind of response would have accomplished two things. It would have acknowledged that, yes, bodies come in all shapes and sizes, and that's okay - while simultaneously noting that there is so much more to a person than what we can visually observe, and urging Tristan to turn his attention to those things, instead.

Thin bodies, fat bodies, bodies of all sorts of shapes and sizes - *none* of them need to be commented on. Period. At the end of the day, after all, we're all just people, wearing our people suits. And there's *so* much more to talk about than the suits.

Here - I'll even prove it.

COMPLIMENTS THAT ARE NOT BODY-CENTRIC

- Positive energy and/or outlook
- Leadership skills
- Magnetic personality
- A contagious laugh
- A bright smile
- Skills and talents
- Self-awareness
- Willingness to help others
- Achievements and successes
- Acts of kindness

Spend a day trying this out, and you may be surprised at what you learn about others. So often, we limit our observations to what we can *see*, meaning we don't pay nearly as much attention to the stuff that actually makes others who they are. By making a point to look deeper, you may find yourself connecting with people on a much more intimate and fulfilling level, which is super satisfying and can form stronger bonds and relationships with others. Talk about a positive impact on our lives!

And, because young minds are so impressionable, it's important that our interactions with the children in our lives acknowledge body positivity *and* don't make the visual observation of bodies the main topic of conversation.

If, like me, you often feel awkward around young children and find yourself defaulting to body talk just to have *something* (anything!) to say, refer to this list for conversational topics that have nothing to do with physical attributes of any kind and instead get to the heart of who someone really is.

THINGS TO DISCUSS WITH KIDS THAT ARE NOT BODY-CENTRIC

- Their favorite subject in school
- Where in the world they most want to visit
- Their favorite animal, and why
- Their hobbies
- Their friends
- Their favorite memory
- The funniest person they know
- Their role models
- Their most desired super power

- Their favorite holiday
- All the cool things they want to do someday

These are the conversations that really get us to open up to one another and connect on a deeper level - and *these* are the conversations that will leave our fellow humans feeling good about who they are, not just how they look.

- 4 -

How Did We Get Here?

It's no secret that we as a society are obsessed with fat: with hating it, with losing it, with calling out people who have an excess of it, or more of it than they used to. With fearing it, with loathing it, with avoiding it at all costs.

Though most of us are at least vaguely aware of this, not everyone sees it as a problem. This is indicative of a pervasive and deep-seated illness that exists in our culture - an illness that was born out of the oppressive systems of misogyny, capitalism and classism and that many of us lack the ability to even *see*.

I grew up in a house with an underground sprinkler system in the backyard. Lots of people in my neighborhood had them, and having only known a way of life in which sprinkler systems were abundant, it never occurred to me that there was any other way. It wasn't until my early twenties, when I moved to a far more humid region of the U.S., that it even dawned on me that irrigation systems for lawns were a very climate-specific tool, and that not every home came equipped with one. It made perfect sense - it's just that I'd never *thought* about it. I'd never considered another way.

By the same token, the vast majority of us, having grown up in a culture that abhors fat and fatness, are blind to the fact that *we don't have to live this way.* Just as not every lawn needs irrigation, we don't *need* strict rules about the ways in which human beings should look - but we're so used to them, we don't stop to question why they're actually there. We so rarely think about the fact that modern beauty standards are *created* - by a handful of industries, no less, that make billions upon billions of dollars peddling prejudice and hatred.

That's right, my friends. We didn't just *evolve* to hold negative opinions about fatness - we hold negative opinions about fatness because we have been *trained* to. The enforcement of beauty standards is nothing but a business model, and it's profiting off our own self-loathing and putting all sorts of prejudice and negativity into the world - like those big factories that spew toxic black smoke into the air and make it hard for anyone to breathe.

JUST HOW BAD IS IT?

Here we are, having come to accept the hatred of fat bodies as the norm. Can we just take a moment to acknowledge how odd that is? Fatness has no bearing on strength of character or moral aptitude. It tells us nothing about a person's skills, loves, successes, or personality traits. There is literally *nothing* about possessing ample amounts of fat that should lead anyone to the conclusion that fat folks are deserving of societal hatred.

Sadly, though, being fat is widely regarded as one of the worst things a person can be. Consider the results of a group of studies[2-3], performed from 2006 to 2011, about people's perception of fatness as utterly despicable. Out of those surveyed, 46% said they would rather give up one year of their lives than be obese. And a staggering 15% were willing to trade ten years of their lives - *ten years* - in favor of the knowledge they'd never be obese.

Think of everything you could do in ten years. Create a masterpiece, travel the world, fall in love, start a family, build an entrepreneurial empire. Picture ten priceless years with the people you love most - your spouse, your children, your best friend, your parents, your siblings. Think about where you were ten years ago, and how much has happened since - *really* get a feel for how long that is.

Now, think about the fact that 15% of people would be willing to trade all of that time and all of the experiences that could fit inside it, in order to ensure they'd never get fat.

Damn, you guys.

What about one year? Take a moment to reflect on the last twelve months, and *alllllll* the things you did during them. Think of the simple pleasures: crawling into a cozy bed at the end of a long day, hugging those you love, making someone laugh, listening to your favorite music, sipping a hot beverage, making art, making love, driving with the windows down, smelling the air after a spring rain, cooking a nice meal, getting lost in a good book, doing something kind for someone, binge-watching cat videos on YouTube...the list goes on and on, but the fact of the matter is that these are the moments that truly make life worth living - and these are the moments that *almost half the population* would opt to sacrifice for the promise of a certain type of body.

Keep in mind, too, that the survey wasn't offering up the promise of bodily perfection, or even specifically *thinness* - solely the *avoidance* of obesity. People literally believe that an earlier death is a favorable alternative to double chins and plus-size clothing.

What the fuck.

It makes me want to weep, or vomit, or maybe both.

If a genie popped out of a lamp and offered the promise that I'd look like a Victoria's Secret model for the rest of my life, but that the price was a tiny portion of my time on earth, I'd tell that genie to kindly fuck off, thank you very much. I wouldn't give even one day of my life - not one *minute* - to look a certain way. Because in that last minute of my life, I'm not going to be thinking about my cellulite or lamenting all the size two dresses I never got to wear. I'm going to be reflecting on what a gift my life has been - how very, very precious it all was - and feeling like the luckiest woman who ever lived. I'm going to go out basking in gratitude and love - and no promise of physical perfection is *ever* worth that price.

Regardless, not everyone, it seems, shares my opinion. There are other ailments and negative situations people view as favorable alternatives to obesity, too. Nearly one-third of survey respondents stated they'd rather have their marriage end in divorce than be fat, and 25% said they'd rather be infertile than plus-size. A quarter of respondents noted that severe depression (the kind that makes even getting out of bed a struggle) would be preferable to fatness, and nearly 15% would rather lose their sense of sight and live the rest of their lives in blindness, unable to even *see* their own bodies.

I know these are just numbers on a page, but I find the statistics truly appalling. Life, love, family, happiness, the ability to observe this beautiful world we live in - these are all things people would willingly surrender *in order to avoid existing inside a fat body.*

I've said it before, and I'll say it again: what the *fuck.*

How bad is it? It's *that* bad.

THE SHADY BUSINESS OF BEAUTY

The diet and weight loss industry in the United States is a $66 billion behemoth - an enterprise devoted to pointing out all the ways in which we are allegedly falling short, under the guise of encouraging "healthier" lives. Looked at in tandem with the $84 billion cosmetic and skin care industry, it's easy to see why the vast majority of us are convinced we aren't enough.

The sad truth is that beauty insecurity is a money-making machine, and businesses will do everything they can to foster such insecurity in favor of their bottom line. A 2017 survey[4] of 3,000 American women between the ages of 16 and 75 revealed that the average woman in their study used $8 worth of cosmetic and skincare products *every day* on her face alone. Taking into account this 60-year age span, this means those women could spend an average of $175,000 on cosmetics in their lifetimes - a figure that can skyrocket up to $300,000 with the addition of splurges, extras, and premium products. Additionally, the survey found that the majority of women used a minimum of *sixteen* products on their faces before leaving the house! Cleansers, toners, serums, eye creams, moisturizers, primers, concealers, foundations, blushers, bronzers, shadows, liners, mascaras, lipsticks... feeling overwhelmed yet? Because I sure am.

What about the weight loss industry? The vast majority of American women have been on at least one diet at some point in their lives, and many of them have dieted consistently since their teenage years. Girls begin dieting at younger and younger ages; currently, the average age for a girl to go on her first diet is *eight*.[5]

Why do we diet? We believe it works - but the truth is that it rarely does. In fact, statistics show that only 3 to 5% of people who diet actually keep the weight off.[6] In fact, more often than not, dieting actually makes us fatter; in 2006, the Journal for the American Dietetic Association published findings that dieting is actually a *risk factor* for obesity! And numerous studies[7] have confirmed that weight-cycling - that is, losing and regaining weight repeatedly over a period of months, years, or a lifetime, also known as yo-yo-dieting - is actually *worse* for one's health than to maintain a state of obesity throughout one's life. Yet there is no shortage of people who will proclaim, to anyone who will listen, that their disdain for fat bodies is due to a deep concern about other peoples' *health*. (More on this in Chapter 5: Stigma & Shame.)

This, then, is why the weight loss industry is still in business: because *diets don't work*. If they did, everyone would get thin and the companies peddling their life-changing programs would quickly have to close up shop. Fad diets throughout the years have aimed to promote "health" by inventing all manner of ridiculous food restrictions. The grapefruit diet, the cabbage soup diet, the "master cleanse" of nothing but lemon juice, cayenne pepper and maple syrup - and these aren't even the strangest or most extreme.

Ever heard of the Sleeping Beauty diet? This gem consists of simply loading up on sedatives so you will sleep right through your starvation - up to 20 hours of artificial slumber a day. Never mind the fact that you're consuming ridiculous amounts of potentially habit-forming drugs and spending your life in a pharmaceutically-induced sleep.

Other diet crazes have taken off throughout the decades. Teenage girls take up smoking cigarettes as an alternative to snacking - because apparently lung cancer is preferable to love handles. Pills full of tapeworm eggs are illegally imported from Central and South American countries so consumers can host the parasite in their bodies as a weight loss plan - a plan that can have serious and even fatal consequences. A few select doctors offer the implantation of tongue patches, making chewing painful and restricting the patient to a liquid diet until the patch is surgically removed a month later. There's even a diet that involves the insertion of a feeding tube through a patient's nose and into the stomach. The tube stays in place for ten days, during which time the patient receives a slow drip of a protein-rich substance totaling 800 calories a day.

And the cotton ball diet - don't even get me started on the cotton ball diet. It's just as it sounds: the dieter dips cotton balls in juice, then *eats* them to quell hunger. The issues with this diet are myriad, and it comes with serious potential health complications. Since the body cannot digest cotton, it remains in the digestive tract and can cause intestinal blockage, which can lead to death. Cotton balls are treated with bleach and contain dioxins, which have been found to cause hormone imbalance, developmental problems, reproductive issues, and cancer. And of course, there's good old malnutrition, due to eating cotton instead of food rich in the vitamins and minerals we all need to survive. Malnutrition is another potentially life-threatening condition.

The common denominator with all these dangerous fad diets? *Starvation.* This, we are told, is the price for physical attractiveness and, by extension, human worth. This is what we must do, because "skinny" is "healthy."

While it's true that most diets aren't quite so extreme, they all rely on some form or another of food restriction, and the vast majority of them will *not* result in long-term weight loss, but rather a lifetime of yo-yo dieting and weight cycling, which, as I mentioned earlier, can actually *cause* obesity. A dieter's greatest fear, realized by...dieting.

Each of these fads and beauty products promises something: youth, vitality, a flatter stomach, a thigh gap, firmer skin, wrinkle reduction. And the underlying message?

You are inadequate. You need to be "fixed." Your flaws need "covered up."

You are not enough.

This is what they're selling. Self-doubt, perceived inadequacy, and low self-esteem - wrapped up in pretty packages touting empty promises of unattainable perfection.

And because money is king, the beauty industry keeps inventing more physical inadequacies for us to focus on, then selling us products to correct them. Highlighter? Contour? Those weren't around when I was sixteen years old – at least, not where I shopped – but now they're all over the beauty aisles at every department store. Are we really that much uglier?

Or are we being had?

My money's on the latter.

MEDIA MATTERS

If the job of the beauty and weight-loss industries is to sell us products to compensate for our physical shortcomings, it's the media's onus to give us something to strive for - a model of perfection that we should struggle to attain at all costs.

The trouble is, these ideals set forth by the media are anything but realistic, which means most of us are chasing goals that, due to genetic makeup, *we can't even reach.*

Take a look at the body type of the models splashed all over television, magazines, and billboards - all flat stomachs, tiny waists, full breasts, curvy posteriors, and thigh gaps. This is what we're told we need to strive for - but what many people don't realize is that this body type is only actually attainable by *five percent* of women. This vast overrepresentation of a widely unrealistic body type has the other 95% of women all over the country despairing over their perceived inadequacies and wondering what's wrong with them and why they can't seem to look like those models, no matter what they do. Is it any wonder so many resort to dangerous weight-loss measures?

And then, there's Photoshop. Suddenly, in the digital age, even the most exquisite women in the world aren't quite perfect *enough*, so their images get the treatment: a pinch in at the waist, a slimming of the thighs, an elongation of the legs. We all know it happens - yet there seems to be a disconnect, because most of us don't think about the fact that the body we are trying so hard to have *doesn't even exist.* It is a composite; an artist's rendering. It's an amalgam of objectification and unrealistic standards, made to look like something physically attainable, if only we just *try* hard enough.

The joke's on us, because the vast majority of us will never get there - but we keep trying anyway. We keep on buying the meal plans, the fad diets, the magical serums, the weight-loss pills, the waist trainers. We keep on going under the knife. We keep on starving our bodies. We keep on spending an exorbitant amount of money for products that will make us appear younger, smaller, firmer, smoother - and for what?

For a super-sized helping of shame when the aforementioned product doesn't magically make us look like Kate Moss. And how do we deal with the shame? We buy more shit that, once again, promises youth, beauty, thinness...

It's like I said: the joke's on us. And the weight loss and beauty giants are the ones laughing - and lining their wallets at our expense.

WE CAN PERPETUATE THE CYCLE... OR WE CAN BREAK IT

While I believe that we are all victims of the media and the multi-billion dollar industries that sell us on hating ourselves, this doesn't let us off the hook. On the contrary! I believe it's on us - all of us - to start paying attention to how *we* perpetuate these harmful ideals, often without even being aware of it.

I've already discussed how thinking of "fat" as a bad word can be incredibly damaging, to adults and kids alike. How else do we unwittingly play into the system?

Full disclosure: this requires a lot of self-exploration, which can be difficult. It's *hard* to take accountability for problematic things we've said or done! But that doesn't give us an excuse not to own up to them. I'm certainly no exception. I've said *so much* problematic shit over the years - just as we all have, because we were born into, and raised within, a problematic culture. It's not our fault - but it *is* our responsibility to recognize it for what it is, and to stop perpetuating it.

As much as I advocate for body positivity today, I used to completely buy into society's harmful notions about appearance. On more than one occasion, I have been guilty of noticing a fat woman in a crop top, for example, and whispering conspiratorially to my friends - and believe me, I'm cringing *so hard* admitting this - "Just because it comes in your size doesn't mean you should wear it." And my friends and I would laugh at the expense of this person who was, in retrospect, a hell of a lot more enlightened than any of us, because it takes some goddamn *strength* to just wear what you want, haters be damned.

I *hate* that I used to say that. But I can't go back in time and fix it, so instead, I've made a decision to learn from it, and to not let it happen again. *This* is the work. This is accountability. It doesn't mean we won't mess up - I still catch myself in problematic thinking patterns from time to time, as does anyone else who was raised in a problematic culture - but it *does* ensure that when you do mess up, you will be willing to step up, examine your words and/or actions, own your part in perpetuating harmful standards, and resolve to do better next time.

What about criticizing our own bodies in front of our children, or other people's children? This is something most of us have done at one point or another, and while it seems fairly harmless, keep in mind that kids are keen listeners, and they pick up on *everything*. When I was growing up, I spent a lot of time around adults who constantly berated the size and shape of their bodies. "I look gross in these jeans." "I feel so fat today." "Time to diet again - I want to be able to wear a swimsuit this summer." I heard these messages on a regular basis, and I internalized them. I grew up thinking it was completely *normal* to bemoan our appearances, punish ourselves with food restriction, and not allow ourselves to wear certain clothing items. Remember the underground sprinkler system I mentioned at the beginning of this chapter? *Negative body talk* was an underground sprinkler system to me. I never thought about why it was there - I just assumed it was the same for everyone. I assumed it was just how things were.

Look, it's no one's *fault*. I can't blame those adults for their negative body talk, just as they can't blame the adults *they* learned it from. We were all raised with this sort of thing as the norm. And deviating from this norm isn't so much about apportioning blame as it is about *breaking the cycle*. Be mindful of how you talk about your body, especially if there are young people with impressionable minds present.

My dear friend and fellow body-positivity advocate Victoria Benjamin shared with me a story about how she realized her own poor self-image had the potential to harm her children.

"I have struggled with my weight for years. When I looked into mirrors, I often thought of myself in terms of *fat* or *disgusting*. Sometimes, I said these things out loud," she told me. "One day, I was at home looking into my bathroom mirror. I noticed my two oldest daughters staring at me, as they often do. I realized that these little girls, who are so beautiful and full of potential, are frequently told they look like *me*. Constant self-critique of my appearance sends the message that they - like me - are ugly, fat, and undeserving of love." Victoria began parenting through a body-positive and inclusive lens, and her children are now some of the most compassionate, confident, and enlightened kids I've ever had the pleasure of knowing. While they received harmful messages in the past, those messages were intercepted early enough that the cycle of self-hatred has been interrupted, making them much less likely to engage in harmful behaviors and attitudes toward their appearances - and the appearances of others - in the future.

"Mothers are often the first - and most influential - example of womanhood for our daughters," Victoria says. "We can mitigate the hell out of self-hatred that may manifest in our children if we could only learn to love ourselves."

Damn straight.

Be mindful, also, of how you talk about *other* people's bodies in the presence of children. Rule number one: just *don't do it*. As we discussed in the previous chapter, this sends the message that A) people are always scrutinizing your body,

.

and B) you are defined by how you look - both of which are harmful.

Marisa, an athlete and veterinary technician, knows this all too well. "My family has always been naturally thin, on both sides. And my mother was very active and stayed fit. She didn't complain about her body, or mine - but she often commented about other people. Things like 'She should *not* be wearing that,' whispered with a wink and nudge, inviting me to join in. And of course I did - it was what I knew. I'm still working to shed those judgmental attitudes about other people. I hope someday I can let them go completely. I don't want to be like that."

What else did you learn in childhood about bodies and physical appearance that you took as truth? I've spoken with so many women who have told me that, growing up, their mothers never left the house without a full face of makeup. Consequently, most of these women now do the same thing.

"It was unheard of - my mom leaving the house without a full paint job," said Lauryn, a retail shop owner who struggles with her body image. "And I didn't even question it - it was like, *of course* a naked face was unacceptable. Now, all these years later, and I still at least put foundation and mascara on every time I leave the house, even if it's just to walk my dog! I hate it, but at the same time, I can't seem to break free. I feel hideous without my mask on."

How sad is it - how utterly heartbreaking - that these insecurities and judgments have so much power to persist through generations, like weeds taking root in a lawn and reappearing year after year? By buying into the fat-phobic ideals that have been sold to us for decades, we are unwittingly spreading the seeds of the insecurities that plague us the most.

It's not about being perfect - just about being honest and admitting where we can do better. It's about owning up to our mistakes and doing our best not to let them happen again. It's about letting go of the harmful things we learned in the past and instead moving forward toward a future in which we can all feel beautiful and confident in our bodies - no matter their shape or size.

- 5 -

Stigma & Shame

When I was in middle school, the very first version of the computer game The Sims was released, and I was given the software as a birthday present. I loved it; there was something so intoxicating about designing my very own houses, neighborhoods, people. It was playing God in a way I never had before, and I spent many happy hours in front of the family computer, building my alternate world.

The options for designing each Sim were limitless, and the characters I created were white, brown, black, male, female, blonde, brunette, and redheaded, but one thing remained constant - my artistic brand, as it were. The women were always, *always* as impossibly thin as the software would allow.

I wondered why there was even an option to make a fat Sim. (*Fat* being entirely subjective, here; the top end of the Sims body type range at the time was no more than a moderate extension of the gut, thighs and posterior, rather than an actual representation of real human fatness.) Who would *want* a character like that? Why create someone so imperfect when you could just as easily make her look like a supermodel?

I never made a fat character - that is, until I grew bored with the storyline I was playing and devised a plan to kill someone off. (In my defense, a quick Google search will reveal that helping Sims reach their untimely ends was, and still is, a popular method of gameplay. Just in case you were wondering if I was a young Hannibal Lecter.)

However, I'd grown attached to my beautiful horde of perfectly exquisite cyber-people, so I realized I needed to create a new character - someone I wouldn't feel bad about shamelessly murdering in a kitchen fire. With the knowledge that I was bestowing upon her an untimely death, I set about making her utterly terrible - mean, lazy, and slovenly. But still, she wasn't enough of a villain to deserve death, so I navigated to the menu that allowed the user to determine a Sim's body type.

That's right. I made her fat - a previously unprecedented choice. *I literally only ever created a fat Sim so that I could kill it,* which really tells you all you need to know about my childhood beliefs surrounding fatness and fat bodies.

I wasn't a fat kid.

However, I lived in fear of becoming fat.

I'd internalized all the social and cultural messages about fatness, the way we all do, and I firmly believed that getting fat was one of the worst things that could happen to a person. I'd seen all the cartoons and movies - I knew damn well that obese people were also, by extension, stupid, sloppy, lazy, and dull. This is how fatness is portrayed in children's media - still - and my beliefs echoed what I saw. Whatever befell me in my life, I vowed, I would never "let myself go" like that.

I can recall, to this day, the exact situation - the exact *moment* - in which I crossed over the threshold. One minute, I was a happy-go-lucky ten-year-old - and the next? A piece of my childhood fell away.

It was during recess in the fifth grade, and I was standing in a patch of grass with a couple of my friends, probably - let's be honest - discussing Pogs. (I'd been tipped off to the growing trend during a recent family visit to California, and as everything on the west coast seemed to happen about three to six months earlier, my cousin pointed out that if I stocked up on the little cardboard discs and brought them back home, my status as a trendsetter would be seriously elevated. Sure enough, by the time whispers of the fad reached Colorado, I already had a burgeoning collection, complete with not just one, but *four* slammers of varying weight and composition, and was thus regarded as something of a goddess in my classroom. My timing had granted me a Cool Kid pass, if only until they became readily available in the area, and I was greatly enjoying my newfound popularity.)

Anyway, there I was that day, talking with my friends, when another one of our classmates approached us. She was a short, skinny girl who'd been spending recess running up to various kids and attempting to lift them off the ground, and she clearly wasn't done yet. She threw her arms around my torso and struggled to pick me up. When she found she couldn't, an expression of scorn danced across her face, and she laughed, as though in pity, and said, "You need to lose some weight."

DID I?!?!? It was the first I'd heard of it, but suddenly I felt like everyone was staring at me. My panic overtook any rationale I may have had on the subject. Now, with the benefit of hindsight and maturity, I see how ridiculous it all was. I was just *larger* than she was. This girl looked like she'd blow away in a strong wind, and I, though not yet overweight, was always a fairly sturdy, bigger-boned kid - but logic, as we know, often has no place in these childhood moments that shape us.

When the bell rang, signaling the end of recess, I went inside and sat down at my desk. I noticed, in horror, the way my thighs spread out when I settled my weight on the chair. *She's right,* I realized.

Thus began twenty years of dieting, starving, bingeing, calorie-counting, fervently wishing I had the willpower to be severely anorexic, and otherwise believing that my body was simply not good enough.

I went on my first diet several months later, at the ripe old age of eleven. I'd grown very aware of my body since the incident on the playground, having started my period and suddenly graduated from girlhood into a full-fledged, card-carrying woman, if all the books I read about "my changing body" were to be believed. I'd begun noticing the ideal feminine figure - how could I avoid it, when it was all over television and magazines? And in comparing those bodies to my own, I was not at all surprised but still dismayed to learn they looked nothing alike.

Some of my classmates, I noticed, were beginning to look like those perfect women. They had slender waists, long legs, petite bones, dainty hands and feet. By comparison, I felt clunky and oafish. My butt stuck out too far. My belly had a slight outward curve to it. My thighs were too thick. Even my feet were wide and ungainly, my toes chubby-looking stumps. I took to stripping naked and examining myself in the bathroom mirror, looking for every possible flaw. The more I did this, the more disgusted with myself I felt - yet I couldn't seem to stop.

For years, I carried this burden of shame around on my back. And as my weight fluctuated drastically as an adult, the shame never waned in congruence. No matter the number on the scale, the self-hatred was always, always there.

THE SCARLET LETTER

Being fat is like wearing a scarlet letter, except instead of just the letter, it's your whole body. Under scrutiny, *alllll* the time.

There's no hiding it. No amount of clothing can cover it. Everywhere you go, everyone knows what you are.

I believe it's a verifiable fact that every one of us has something we are painfully insecure about. And the reality of life for so many fat people is that the thing we're most insecure about is right out in the open, for everyone to see.

It can be extraordinarily limiting. I didn't set foot in a gym for years, for example, because I could always feel countless sets of judgmental eyes burning holes in the back of my head - or, more accurately, my ass, as it wobbled and bounced and swayed on the treadmill. I'd been trained to believe that, as a fat person, I should take up permanent residence inside the gym until I was significantly smaller - but even there, in the place I was *supposed* to be in order to fix the problem that was my body, I felt horribly alienated and ashamed.

One of my favorite things to do has always been to take myself out for dinner. This certainly isn't everyone's cup of tea, but I love it. It's an opportunity to sit back, observe, listen, read, write, or do whatever it is I feel like doing, all while enjoying a delicious meal. I never thought twice about this when my body was of a more socially palatable size. Now, though, there's always that nagging voice in my head: *people will think you're here by yourself because you're fat and sad and alone and looking to drown your feelings in food. Eat up, Miss Piggy.*

Of course, it doesn't *matter* what people think, and I do my best to squash that voice down into the dirt as soon as it makes its presence known. But it's still there. It's still a marked difference in those dining experiences, and I can't help but notice it.

There are many things I find myself doing differently now that I am fat, usually centering around food. After all, for a thin person, eating is perfectly acceptable. But for a fat person? Unless they're taking delicate bites of a petite salad - dressing on the side, of course - their food choices are often scrutinized by the people around them.

I'll never forget one particular morning, on the way to work at my old job. I'd left early and stopped at a small breakfast place for a cup of coffee and a bagel sandwich, fueling up for the day ahead. Sitting in a booth, I tucked into my meal. The sandwich was overly messy, and as I've never been known for my tidiness, I managed to inadvertently smear cream cheese all over the side of my face. I felt the goop on my cheek and reached for a pile of napkins, and as I did so, I made eye contact with a woman sitting at a nearby table. She looked at me with such disdain - disgust, even - that I felt my stomach drop. Her eyes traveled from the cream cheese on my cheek, down to my full upper arms and the mountain of my belly disappearing beneath the tabletop. I'd *revolted* her - and the body scan she so obviously did made it very clear that it wasn't just my messiness that had done it, but the fact that I was a fat slob eating a fattening meal.

With my cheeks burning in shame, I looked away, then wished I hadn't. It felt uncomfortably like I'd let her win - like I'd conceded, somehow. But I hadn't known what else to do. What is the protocol, after all, for when you're eating and someone you don't know stares at you as though you're a zoo animal tucking into this morning's slop? It's dehumanizing. It's *horrible*.

So many fat people experience such shame around food that it's as though we're trying to keep up this pretense that we don't actually eat at all. Even after all the work I've done to be comfortable inside my plus-size body, I still find myself following certain rules around food that I've set for myself, usually unconsciously. For example, I do my best to stay away from fast food, but every so often, I cave and hit up a drive-through, usually if I'm in a rush on the way to a meeting or appointment. And to this day, I still tuck the garishly identifiable paper bag beneath the passenger seat of my car until I can dispose of it in the privacy of my own home. Because heaven forbid someone sees an empty Taco Bell bag sitting on my front seat. I don't want to be a cliché. After all, they're not supposed to know I eat.

Same applies for while I'm eating. If I've stopped at a light and a car pulls up beside me, I'll promptly lower my sandwich, or whatever it is I'm enjoying, so that no one can see me eating it, only resuming my meal when we're all driving again and no one has time to watch me.

As a fat person, there are things you shouldn't do and places you don't belong - everyone knows this. I've seen people do double-takes as I walk into a health food store or try to hide their incredulity as I leave the gym. *You don't belong here.* If I'm ever out in public and decide to dance, I just sort of automatically know that there will be people making fun of the way I look, flinging my fatness around the dance floor. *You shouldn't be doing that.*

As I said, just about everyone has something we're insecure about. But when that something is on display for the whole world to see, it's a very different experience altogether.

WHAT ARE WE SO ASHAMED OF?

I've always loved music, and in my free time, I enjoy writing songs, singing, and playing my guitar. Several years ago, I had a friend who purported himself to be my "biggest fan." He lived a few states away, and he would often call me in the evenings and ask me to play songs for him. I was overwhelmed by his support; I'd never really believed wholeheartedly in my musical abilities, but he insisted I had what it took to *make it*.

Except for one thing.

"You know," he said to me one night on the phone, "You're really talented. I seriously think people would love your songs. But…"

"But what?" I asked.

"Well," he said, matter-of-factly, "I'm sure you know this already, but just to make sure…you're going to have to lose a *lot* of weight if you ever want to really succeed in the music industry."

I didn't know what to say. On the one hand, I believed, there was logic to what he was telling me. On the other, I couldn't get over how unspeakably *rude* it was for him to give voice to such a thought. Looking back, I wish I'd given him ten kinds of hell. I wish I'd made him feel like shit. But all that ended up happening was that *I* felt like shit, because amidst all the emotional confusion about sorting out my feelings, my response was flimsy and weak.

"I know, I guess - I mean, yeah, I know I'm heavy and all, but it's not *impossible* to succeed at my size…"

"Oh, you may have a hit or two at first," he carried on confidently, blithely unaware of my discomfort. "But you won't have staying power. Why do you think Adele has fallen off the map?"

I just sat there, opening and closing my mouth like a fish, unsure as to what was actually happening. *Had* Adele fallen off the map? It was the first I'd heard of it. As far as I knew, she'd just had a kid and was enjoying family life, while reveling in the smashing success of her award-winning albums *19* and *21*. But what did I know?

"Oh, um - has she?" I replied vaguely, aware that I should say *some*thing.

"Yeah, and it's because no one wants to see *that* onstage. It's just a fact."

Yes. This man, who I considered at the time to be one of my closest and most supportive friends, had tried to convince me that even Adele - the ass-kicking multi-millionaire songstress with no less than *nine* Grammies under her belt at the time of that conversation - was somehow unsuccessful *on account of her size alone.*

And the saddest thing of all is that I actually believed him.

We, as humans, have a large propensity for shame. Arguably, women fall prey to this even more heavily than men; existing in a female body within the patriarchy ensures we'll practically be *born* wearing a backpack full of shame around our bodies and our sexuality. And that backpack only grows as we do. Due to social and cultural conditioning, we're experts at piling shame all over ourselves, flinging it every which way until we're literally buried beneath it.

And in case our *own* self-flagellation wasn't bad enough, there are plenty of people in the world who are willing to take one for the team, step in, and help us hate ourselves. There are two main types of these folks, outlined as follows:

THE FAT-SHAMERS

Fat-shamers think fat people are disgusting, and they won't hesitate to let you know. These are the people who take photos of fat people at the gym and post them online, inviting others to poke fun at the whale on the treadmill. They're the people who record videos of themselves yelling at fat people to just get off their asses already, then post them on YouTube (if you've never seen these, take it on my word that they exist and don't go looking for them yourself, unless you enjoy being made to feel like some kind of grotesque, subhuman smorgasbord of inadequacy and failure). They're the people who'll give you the once-over at a restaurant while you're tucking into your fettuccine alfredo and ask disdainfully "Haven't you had enough?" They're the people who see my articles on the internet, disagree with the content, and subsequently decide that sending me Facebook messages telling me I'm fat and ugly is the correct course of action (obviously).

I haven't personally found these folks to be too prevalent in day to day life, fortunately (although I've heard many accounts from other folks that prove fat-shamers are alive and well just about everywhere), but the internet is crawling with them. They're not just commenting on Facebook - they're running websites and writing books and posting the aforementioned YouTube videos that are viewed tens of thousands of times.

THE CONCERN TROLLS

This sort of shamer is much more common, and a lot harder to spot at a glance. These are the people who say things like "I'm just worried about your health" and "You know you're going to die sooner if you keep eating like that, right?" On the surface, it seems that they care - but digging deeper, their motives become clear.

I've come across many of these concern trolls via the internet, and I find them utterly baffling. It's really *weird* to encounter a random stranger and immediately foster a deep concern for their physical health. When was the last time you made eye contact with someone at the grocery store and thought to yourself, "Golly, I sure hope her kidneys are working properly"? The answer, most likely, is never - yet this certain breed of fat shamer will insist that *they really are that concerned* about your physical well-being, even though they don't actually *know* you. Still, they *care* - so much that they're willing to go out of their way to tell you how disgracefully unhealthy you are, as though they are your personal physician.

I don't know about you guys, but I find it hard to believe that these folks' bleeding hearts keep them up at night, worrying about people they've never even met. And when I post a photo of myself on social media and some random stranger comments "Junk food is unhealthy, you should eat less of it," despite knowing literally nothing about my dietary habits, I am altogether skeptical as to their insistence that they're just making sure I have this information because they *care* about my well-being.

Then, there are the in-real-life people - the friends, family members, colleagues. Typically - at least, in my experience - these are the ones that sting the most. It's easy to write off trolls on the internet. But when someone in your immediate circle keeps insisting to you that you're unhealthy, even when your medical records state otherwise? It hurts, and it's hard to deal with. Making the situation even more difficult is that, most likely, the other person truly believes they are doing you a favor. As though perhaps you didn't realize just how fat and unhealthy you actually are, and now that someone has so graciously pointed it out to you, you'll immediately skip off to the gym, bound and determined to get *healthy*.

A couple years ago, I mentioned a recent doctor's visit to a friend in passing. I don't remember what I'd gone in for - a persistent sore throat or something - but this friend's immediate reaction was, "What did the doctor say about your weight?"

I was taken aback. "Uh...we didn't talk about it. It wasn't relevant." (I consider myself *very* lucky indeed to have a physician who doesn't automatically prescribe weight loss to cure a vast array of ailments, from earaches to a sprained elbow to appendicitis.)

And then came the dreaded statement: "I'm just worried about your health." The insinuation being, of course, that my size automatically meant I was unhealthy - as though the existence of lots of fat on my body meant that I was probably ready to kick the bucket, right then and there.

SHAMED INTO CHANGE?

The people who shame fat folks may have the best of intentions. There are lots of those out there who truly believe that the more a person is shamed into losing weight, the more likely they are to start a diet, hit the gym, and *do it*. Statistically, however, the opposite is true. Research[8] has shown that the worse we feel about our bodies, largely due in part to shaming and size discrimination, the *less* likely we are to engage in regular physical activity and habitually eat a balanced, nutritious diet - not the other way around. Sure, we may jump on the latest dieting bandwagon and lose a bit of weight, but it won't be long before, frustrated, we return to our old habits once more, regaining every pound we lost (and a few more for good measure). Shame is *not* the way to bring about healthy, positive change; instead, it's more likely to *cause* obesity in those being shamed, rather than the other way around.

But all those fat shamers out there are just worried about our health…right?

THE TRUTH ABOUT HEALTH

Healthy - such a loaded word in this day and age. "Healthy is the new skinny" is the mantra of so many self-proclaimed fitspiration gurus all over the interwebs, usually thin, toned, and enthusiastic. And there's nothing *wrong* with wanting to be healthy. In and of itself, health is an excellent thing to strive for.

We encounter problems, however, when these bubbly fitness experts (or, in some cases, "experts") take it upon themselves to use weight as a proxy for health. This doesn't do us any favors. This is, in fact, the same damn thing as peddling thinness as the ultimate goal. Skinny, healthy, whatever you want to call it - it's still an ideal we're told to strive for, using the *appearance of one's body* as a barometer. This is where the notion of health is so flawed. It is impossible to determine the health of another human being simply by observing the shape of their body. Moreover, when we say things like "healthy is the new skinny," we are ascribing a certain moral weight to health - as though if you're *not* healthy, you are somehow *less than*.

This can be especially exclusionary for people with chronic health issues or disabilities. If we are constantly being met with messages that health is the most important thing we can have, where does that leave folks who fall outside the circle? Marginalized and oppressed, that's where.

While it is true that obesity has been correlated with certain health risks, research shows that there is not always adequate cause for such associations. Most of us, for example, have heard the frightening claim that obesity shortens lives. In her enlightening book *Body of Truth*, Harriet Brown describes the genesis of one such argument, published in an article by S. Jay Olshansky of the University of Illinois at Chicago. Olshansky's claim was that rising obesity rates would shave two to five years off of human lifespans. Like a spark giving way to a wildfire, that statistic was repeated and shared throughout many other journals and media outlets, and before long, Americans were being told that, for the first time in history, a generation of children would have shorter lifespans than their parents - a statement that simply *wasn't true*. David B. Allison, one of Olshansky's co-authors, even *admitted* the lack of evidence for the claim, calling their findings mere "back-of-the-envelope plausible scenarios" and stating, "We never meant for them to be portrayed as precise."

Yet this claim, and so many others like it, *are* being portrayed as precise: mere projections and pondering, delivered to us as cold, hard truth. Why? Why are we so invested in the belief that fatness and unhealthiness are essentially one and the same?

You may be surprised - or not - to learn that so much of it boils down to...

Money.

That's right - as it turns out, spreading misinformation about weight and health is highly profitable for those with their fingers in the right pies. Weight-loss surgery centers, pharmaceutical companies, diet enterprises, and even some medical professionals have lots to gain by perpetuating exaggerated and misleading information.

Take, for example, the United Kingdom's National Obesity Forum, who admitted to *lying* in a report about the projection for obesity among British citizens. The report gave intentionally misrepresented "facts," portraying a large rise in obesity when the research stated otherwise. Why? The NOF is a lobbying organization that just so happens to be in bed with an impressive list of pharmaceutical companies - companies who would benefit from an increase in weight-loss medication prescriptions. But surely that's a coincidence?

Sadly, it's not. Shortly after an update to the U.S. Dietary Guidelines was released in 2015, an article[9] published in Time Magazine presented evidence that the new guidelines had little to do with changes in nutritional needs... and everything to do with financial and political gain. Despite claims from the USDA that these guidelines are "grounded in the most current scientific evidence," many leading experts came forward in suspicion of the opposite, stating heavy influence from food manufacturers and special interest groups. We're talking about the guidelines that influence public nutrition programs, school lunch menus, and the shopping lists of millions of Americans, under the premise of helping people make healthy food choices - but it turns out that those guidelines, too, can be bought as long as the price is right.

We've all heard of the "obesity epidemic" - a swift and damning increase in obesity as the years wear on. However, the methodology for measuring obesity has changed over time as well, skewing the numbers and making everything appear much more grim than it actually is. For instance, prior to 1997, the Body Mass Index chart dictated that "overweight" applied to women with a BMI of 27 or above, and men with a BMI of 28 or above. That year, however, a panel of experts (many of whom, interestingly, were later revealed to have deep financial ties to manufacturers of weight loss drugs) voted to lower the cutoff point to 25. From this simple change alone, the percentage of Americans classified as overweight instantly increased by *millions*, despite no actual weight gain among them. When we alter our measures for definition, we alter the statistics, too.

The panel claimed the BMI change was due to the fact that the general public needed a nice, round number - a multiple of five - in order to remember it. A more plausible explanation, however, is the vast array of weight loss services, treatments, and products that newly "overweight" patients were suddenly eligible for. All this, of course, means more money in the pockets of the weight loss industry, pharmaceutical companies, and healthcare providers (including the panel members) who receive kickbacks for patient referrals.

The BMI chart isn't the only area in which the goal posts have been moved. We can see the same clever trickery if we just examine guidelines for pre-diabetes and pre-hypertension classifications, both of which were altered in 2003 to include more and more people in "at risk" groups and, subsequently, profit off their sudden need for medical intervention. Prior to the changes, less than a tenth of all American adults were considered pre-diabetic, and 30 percent were considered to have pre-hypertension. After the shift, those numbers skyrocketed to 40 percent and 60 percent, respectively, though these patients' vital statistics hadn't changed at all.[10] Voila - a pair of brand spanking new epidemics, ready and waiting to line the pockets of those who profit from them.

Meanwhile, legitimate, data-driven, and meticulously researched studies appear from time to time, debunking commonly held beliefs about fat and fatness and suggesting that being overweight isn't actually a death sentence (imagine that). And, perhaps unsurprisingly, when they emerge, they are vilified, denounced, dragged through the mud, picked apart, and deemed highly inaccurate, despite all evidence to the contrary. One such study[11] was published by a group of researchers from the Center for Disease Control, led by epidemiologist Katherine Flegal, in 2013. The study was expected to show that a higher BMI leads to increased mortality rates, but to the surprise of the researchers, their data pointed in a different direction. After years of dedicated data collection and study, the findings stated that being overweight was *not,* in fact, a risk factor for premature death. Additionally, they found that severe obesity increased the chances of premature death only slightly - *significantly* less than had been previously believed.

Of course, when this study was published, it was met with an onslaught of dismissal, disparagement, and outright anger[12] - as though Flegal and her team were the big, fat liars, instead of the other way around.

It should be clear by now that there are many companies, organizations, industries, and even individuals who profit from the stigmatization of fat and fatness. The truth, then, is that we hold such deeply ingrained beliefs about weight and health because we've been *manipulated* into doing so.

HEALTHCARE AND THE WEIGHT BIAS

Recently, I had my yearly physical with my doctor, and the following week, I received a detailed packet in the mail, showing the results from all of my preventative lab work. Everything looked *gorgeous* - so gorgeous, in fact, that I was tempted to take a picture of the letter and share it on the internet, as proof that it is possible for someone to be fat *and also* have excellent blood pressure, cholesterol levels, and cardiovascular function. According to this letter, I am at an exceptionally low risk of heart disease in the foreseeable future - and while I had already known this, I wanted other people to know it, too. *See? I'm fat AND healthy - my doctor says so.*

I even brought up the subject with my doctor once. I'd been seeing her for a couple years and she'd never even insinuated that I needed to lose weight, so I wanted to bring everything onto the table. Was she just keeping the truth from me? Was she being nice to my face, then grimacing at my disgustingness as soon as I left the examination room?

But when I asked her if she thought I should lose weight, she looked me in the eye and said, "Honestly? There's so much more to the picture of your health than the number on the scale. Losing weight probably wouldn't hurt you - but having the weight isn't necessarily hurting you, either. Your vitals and lab work always look great. You're healthy and strong, just as you are. As long as you're eating a nutrient rich diet and getting some kind of physical activity regularly, I'm happy."

I was *shocked.* I had just asked a healthcare professional if I should lose weight, opening the doors for the ugly truth and its subsequent onslaught of shame - and the truth she'd given me hadn't been so ugly, at all.

Our cultural bias toward thinness causes us to make assumptions about people's health based on their appearance - an assessment that's hardly ever accurate. Delia, age 38, suffers from a myriad of health problems: an autoimmune disorder, severe food allergies, and chronic pain, to name a few. She also happens to be thin. "Not once has anyone ever expressed concern for my health based on the way my body looks," she told me, "because my body is conventionally 'correct.' But I'm probably far less healthy than most plus-size people."

The misconception that *thin* means *healthy* is something I've personally experienced, too. In my early twenties, I developed a strange illness that damn near prohibited me from eating food at all. I'd put a bite in my mouth and start to chew, and instantly, before the morsels had even reached my stomach, I'd feel nauseous - the kind of feeling you get when you eat a whole box of chocolate Teddy Grahams in one sitting and then realize you seriously might vom. (What, *me?* Never.)

I saw doctors. I got tested for food allergies, Chron's disease, and celiac sprue. Everything came back negative. According to the professionals, I was in perfect health - except for the minor inconvenience of not being able to feed myself. While this concerned me a great deal, none of the doctors I saw seemed particularly upset about it, a fact I can only attribute to my fatness.

"Look on the bright side," they'd say with a shrug. "You're losing weight." As though that was the ultimate goal, all symptoms aside. As though I deserved a medal instead of an MRI. Back then, I didn't realize I had a right to be angry and indignant about this dismissal of a very real issue, but if I was treated the same way today, you can be sure I'd raise all kinds of hell.

So I never got any answers, and I continued to eat one or two bites at a time, a few times a day. Just under five months later, I'd lost seventy pounds. That is a ridiculous and fairly unsafe rate of weight loss - but instead of being concerned for my health, people *congratulated* me. Friends and family told me how much better I looked. The guy I was infatuated with said I was getting sexier every day and hinted at the fact that maybe my weight loss meant we could be in a relationship. Not many people seemed to care that I was suffering a very real health issue - on the contrary, they were *happy* for me!

Can we pause just for a moment to observe how heinously *fucked up* that is? Here I was telling people I couldn't physically do something the human body needs to survive and was wasting away as a result - and the resounding response was "Good for you, so glad you're getting healthier!" *Healthier*, they said, during the point in my life when I felt the most *un*healthy. There I was, so weak I could barely even climb a flight of stairs, even losing consciousness more than once after standing up too quickly - and simultaneously being congratulated on my good health. Because, as everyone knows, fat people are unhealthy and thin people are healthy. Simple as that. Right?

It's enough to make a person want to scream.

As I mentioned earlier, I am grateful to have a doctor who refuses to subscribe to stereotypes around weight and health. Unfortunately, my experience isn't common. Weight bias is a very real thing, and despite the hippocratic oath sworn by health care providers, it does much harm, indeed.

The Rudd Center for Food Policy & Obesity, formerly out of Yale University and now operating from the University of Connecticut, has published a vast array of studies and reports on weight bias within the healthcare setting. One such report[13] from 2009 revealed that more than half of primary care physicians described their obese patients as "noncompliant," as well as "awkward," "unattractive," and "ugly." Doctors reported that seeing obese patients was a bigger waste of time than seeing thin patients, and they referred to their heavier patients as "annoying" and predicted that they would be less likely to heed medical advice, based on their size alone.

Another report[14] published in 2012 revealed still more distressing findings from various studies. In a group of nurses surveyed on their attitudes toward obesity, 31 percent said they would prefer not to provide care to obese patients. A quarter of respondents agreed that they were "repulsed" by their heavier patients, with 12 percent going so far as to say they preferred to avoid touching them altogether. Meanwhile, doctors associated obesity with hostility, dishonesty, and poor hygiene.

Even dentists weren't found to be immune from weight stigma; nearly 20% of those surveyed stated that they were uncomfortable treating obese patients, claiming that the larger the patient, the harder it was to feel empathy for them.

Is it so surprising, then, that these studies also revealed that obese people are more likely to delay or forgo preventative care, including cancer screenings, pelvic exams, and mammograms? The lack of utilization of preventive care services only increases among obese patients who have experienced weight-based discrimination or stigmatization from doctors and other health care providers.

There's no shortage of people out there who will tell us, until they're blue in the face, that being fat will make us sick - but correlation does not equal causation. Among a population that is less likely to seek preventive services and screenings *and* given less time face-to-face with a doctor when they do[15], it is quite fair indeed to wonder if the correlation between obesity and disease is due, at least in part, to the weight bias and the subsequent compromise of medical care for obese and overweight patients.

BUT THINK OF THE TAXPAYERS!

A common concern folks have surrounding fatness and fat people is the issue of who will pay for the health care they will undoubtedly need due to their presumably unhealthy bodies. "*My* tax dollars shouldn't go toward paying for *your* heart attack," these people like to parrot. What they are oh-so-conveniently forgetting is that it's not just fat people who need medical care - yet we are so often the ones vilified for it. We, as humans, take risks to our health every single day - every time we cross a street, or climb a ladder, or get into a car. Motor vehicle accidents are a costly burden for the general public; per a study from the United States Department of Transportation[16], public revenues paid for about 7 percent of costs related to automobile accidents in 2010, including medical expenses. This cost U.S. taxpayers $18 billion a year - or more than $156 in added taxes for every household in the country. Yet we don't bring this up every time we see someone get into a vehicle.

Substance abuse is another financial vacuum. A 2016 study from the Surgeon General[17] reported that the yearly economic impact of the misuse of alcohol is a whopping $249 billion - and taxpayers foot the majority of the bill. And don't forget all the cigarette smokers! Nearly $170 billion pays for direct medical care for smoking-related illnesses every year.[18]

Firearm-related injuries in America rack up a $730 billion tab annually[19], and taxpayers foot 41% of the bill. That's nearly $300 billion each year from the pockets of taxpayers - because of our apparent inability to regulate *guns*.

Conversely, it's estimated that obesity-related illnesses - that is, illnesses that are *correlated* with, but not *caused by*, obesity - cost around $150 billion to $200 billion each year.[20] Keep in mind, too, that this is accounting for *all* instances of these illnesses - not just the ones presented by obese patients. Because as we know, thin people can and do suffer heart disease, diabetes, hypertension, and cancer, among other diseases. Fat people are *not* solely responsible for this financial burden - a burden that, it turns out, pales in comparison to our financial losses from booze and guns. Yay, America.

$$\approx$$

What all this means is that we stigmatize fat and fatness because we've been trained to do so. Manipulation and deceit have led to abundant misinformation about weight and health. We're sold on the lie that fat people are a burden to the system and taught that abhorring fatness is a very reasonable and pragmatic thing to do. We've spent our lives marinating in scare tactics and alarmist warnings of risks and epidemics, designed for the sole purpose of making a profit, not making people healthier.

It's long past time to start seeing things for what they *are* - not what special interests want us to *think* they are.

- 6 -

Bodies & the Patriarchy

*"You don't give a shit if a girl can play a
violin like the greatest violinist in the world.
You want to know what does she look like."*
-Donald Trump

In 2013, Heidi Klum, multi-tasking supermodel, actress, and fashion designer, among other roles, was vacationing on the island of Oahu when a riptide nearly claimed the lives of her son, Henry, and the family's nanny. Without thinking, Klum rushed to the rescue; photos from passersby show her surging bravely forward through the rough surf, pulling Henry and the nanny to safety.

However, there was another unexpected element to the photographs: Klum's right nipple, which had slipped free of her bikini top during the rescue.

Naturally, as soon as the story was published, it bore the headline "Heidi Klum Suffers Nip Slip While Rescuing Son And Nanny From Drowning." Yes, you read that right -

the *nip slip* was the focal point of the headline, while all the heroic life-saving stuff was mere context.

To be fair, not *all* the articles about the incident featured the wayward nipple as the main event. But the vast majority at least *mentioned* Klum's breast, or the fact that she made the rescue in nothing but a string bikini. Some aspect of her body was almost always included in the story, no matter which outlet reported on it.

By contrast, just three years later, actor Hugh Jackman rescued his son and some other swimmers from a riptide at Bondi Beach in Sydney, Australia. Unsurprisingly, the commentary about the event focused on Jackman's bravery, strength, and heroism, with no mention of his appearance.

Things like this teach girls, from a young age, that it doesn't matter what we achieve or what awards we win or whose life we save — everyone will still just be scrutinizing our physical forms, because that's what's truly valuable and interesting about us. That's what *really* matters.

Here in the United States, we operate under many oppressive systems: patriarchy, white supremacy, capitalism and colonialism, to name a few. These hierarchies benefit those at the top while giving severe disadvantages to everyone else. And each of them have one major thing in common: the aim to control. Women, people of color, those in the LGBT communities, the differently abled, followers of minority religions, immigrants, and the indigenous - all of these groups have been subjected to the control of our nation's uppermost tier in the privilege hierarchy: white heterosexual cisgender able-bodied Christian men.

A QUICK NOTE ABOUT PRIVILEGE

Privilege is an oft-misunderstood topic, and the cause for so many heated debates in my own life with straight white men who insist that their lack of financial security erases any and all possibility that they hold even the slightest bit of privilege. Because it is so often misinterpreted, I feel it's important for our purposes to establish a basic foundation of what privilege is - and what it is not.

- Privilege is *not* synonymous with wealth. While financial privilege definitely exists, the majority of the different types of privilege have nothing to do with one's net worth.
- Privilege does *not* mean you've had everything handed to you, or that you have not worked hard to get where you are today.
- Privilege is *not* shameful, and having it does *not* make us bad people. No one is asking us to feel guilty because of it.

Simply put, privilege is the notion that, although your life may have been hard, your gender, race, sexual orientation, gender identity, nationality, ability, or body type isn't one of the things making it harder. It's the luxury of not having to worry about something that people in different situations must worry about routinely.

For example, men have the privilege of not having to worry about who slipped what into their drink when they got up to use the restroom, while women have been trained to never leave our drinks unattended.

White people have the privilege of not fearing for our lives when we get pulled over for, say, an expired license plate, while seemingly benign situations like this have proven deadly for people of color.

Heterosexual couples can take the hand of their romantic partner in public without anyone batting an eye; in more conservative areas of the country, same-sex couples still are not afforded this luxury.

Thin people don't have to worry that they won't be able to find a single store that carries clothing in their size.; nor will they have to wonder if the restaurant they'll be visiting for someone's birthday will have chairs they can fit into comfortably. For fat folks, these are very real and common concerns.

These examples show everyday ways in which lack of privilege can complicate lives, adding worry, anxiety, and sometimes even the threat of bodily harm or death. Life is hard enough for everybody - and when you lack privilege in one or more areas, it only gets harder.

Privilege exists in many arenas, including:

- Race (white privilege)
- Gender (male privilege)
- Sexual orientation (straight privilege)
- Gender identity (cis privilege)
- Wealth (financial privilege)
- Religion (Christian privilege)

A person who meets several or all of the above types of privilege falls toward the top of the hierarchy discussed previously, whereas someone who meets few or none of the above will lie toward the bottom.

It's important to note that a lack of privilege in one area does not negate the presence of privilege in another area, or vice versa. Take, for example, a woman of color who is homosexual, transgender, and living with a disability. Let's imagine this woman is also quite wealthy. She can have all the money in the world, but her bank account balance is not going to change the fact that she has the lived experience of specific struggles relating to her gender, race, sexuality, gender identity, and ability. Assuming financial wealth is her only area of privilege, she'll *still* fall farther toward the bottom on the hierarchy.

I am a white woman. My whiteness offers me privilege; my gender does not. I identify with the gender I was assigned at birth, which gives me privilege as well. While I'm certainly not rolling in the dough (not yet, anyway - how's that for putting it out into the universe?), I also know that I have a roof over my head, food to eat, and a car to drive. This gives me privilege over those who do not have those things, but also means I am less privileged financially than someone with a cool million in retirement funds and a beach home in the Hamptons. As a fat person, I do not have privilege with regards to body type, but I am able-bodied and therefore have more privilege than those who are not. These truths are part of my own personal privilege map - a picture of where I stand in relation to the privilege of others - and we can all find out where we stand on that map if we take the time to think about it.

If all this sounds rather complicated, that's because it is! You don't have to be an expert, though, to grasp the concept of privilege and use it to gain a clearer understanding of our culture's social hierarchies. Each of us has our own experience of privilege, and it's on us to own our privilege, wherever it may lie. Again, this isn't about guilt. I can't help that I was born with white skin - but I can acknowledge that because of my white skin, I will never have to deal with certain things that people of color face on a daily basis. When we wake to the areas in which we have privilege, it makes us more likely to listen to those less privileged than us - and makes the world a better place.

Why is this so important? It may seem only loosely connected to body image, but the fact of the matter is that this hierarchy contributes to so much of the world's oppression - and that includes the oppression, and subsequent policing, of women's bodies as a control tactic.

It is, after all, impossible to examine modern beauty standards without discussing our culture's patriarchal roots.

GROWING UP SHE

Looking back on my adolescence, I realize that *every single one* of my female friends expressed some sort of anxiety about the shape of her body - and I was no exception. Every day, we were bombarded with images of the way the female body should look. Of course, the ultimate importance of physical attractiveness had been drilled into our heads practically from birth, and we stared despairingly at our own bodies in the mirror, hating them for what they were and wishing upon everything we held dear to just look different. Thinner, curvier, taller, shorter, prettier...*better*.

An alarming amount of us - myself included - internalized this despair so deeply that we fully believed our self-worth was dictated by it; that we were somehow flawed or incorrect, just by looking the way we did. I have a distinct memory of yearning to take acting classes in high school, but concluding that I simply wasn't thin enough or pretty enough to be a *real* actress. That dream went unpursued.

This is the reality for adolescent girls in America, every single day. And sadly, most of them accept this as the norm; the status quo. It's just how the world is, they rationalize, just as my friends and I did when we were young. *Attractiveness is everything. It's natural.*

Meanwhile, boys of the same age aren't feeling this kind of burden. That's not to say there's *no* burden; maybe they get picked on for being too scrawny or too chubby, which can certainly be damaging. Maybe they deal with body image issues of their own.

But there's a big difference here, and it is that, as males, what they *won't* have to deal with are the constant messages, all around them, that *the thing that matters most about them are their bodies.*

They will hear about men in the media. Men who have triumphed in sports or who have run Fortune 500 companies or who have received recognition in their chosen field. The accomplishments of these men will be highlighted on television, in magazines and on billboards - and there is a good chance that *none of those advertisements will hone in on these men's bodies.* We most likely won't see a zoomed-in photograph of a male CEO's stretch marks, or hear musings on how much weight the latest action movie hero has gained. While it's true that their physical attributes may be mentioned, the underlying *meaning* behind these men - their intrinsic worth as human beings - will *not* be tied in to the diameter of their bellies.

For the girls, however, it's an entirely different experience altogether. TV commercials tell us we need more radiant skin, more lustrous hair, a flatter belly, a tinier waist. We are bombarded with advertisements from cosmetics companies, all designed to send the message that we are not pretty enough in our natural state. We watch as the female body is scrutinized, sexualized, and objectified by just about every aspect of mainstream media. We see these bodies used to sell every product from clothing to jewelry to *fast food hamburgers* - because sex, as we all know, sells.

We learn that if that female body is exposed, the context is *almost always sexual in nature*, reinforcing society's opinion that the female is an inherently sexual creature. We begin to form ideas about our own sexuality, internalizing the idea that being sexually attractive - being *desired* - is the highest honor, the crowning achievement of our lives.

Society trains us by objectifying us - until eventually, we objectify *ourselves*.

When I was nineteen, I went to a party and met a guy there. We talked for a while, and he asked for my phone number. I wasn't particularly interested in him - but I was also fat, and beggars couldn't be choosers. Male attention wasn't something I received often, if at all, so I supposed I'd better at least give it a shot. (Full disclosure: writing the previous two sentences makes me want to time-travel back to the past and shout at my young self, *"Where's your self-respect? You don't need a man! FUCK THE PATRIARCHYYYYY!"* But alas, I was young and entirely ignorant to the deeply-rooted gender roles I was allowing to dictate my behavior.)

He called me a few days later. His name was Matt, and looking back, I think the only reason I liked him at all was because he seemed to like *me*. My self-esteem was painfully low in those days, and I found it difficult to understand how another human being could possibly want to be in a relationship with me. It didn't seem to matter that we had nothing in common. I willfully overlooked his binge drinking, his habitual drug use, and his tendency to steal from the cash register at the bakery where he worked. I even started doing cocaine with him and his friends, in a desperate attempt to belong.

This, right here, is evidence of how we are socially conditioned. The belief that it's better to spend our time with shitty people than to be alone with ourselves is intensely fucked up - and unsettlingly common. When we spend literally a lifetime being brainwashed by our culture into thinking that our physical attributes alone should dictate the quality of our interactions with others, we come to believe we don't deserve any better. It's a recipe for trauma that can haunt us until the day we die - or, at the very least, cause us to settle instead of thrive.

One day, about six months into our "relationship" (if you can call getting fucked up all the time and watching a lot of TV a relationship), Matt and a male friend of mine went out for a beer. Later, I received a phone call from my friend.

"I feel like I should tell you something."

He went on to describe how Matt had confided in him over their pint glasses. "Know why I always pick the fatties?" he'd asked my friend. "Because they're desperate, man! You can do whatever you want and they'll never leave."

To say hearing this broke my heart would be an exaggeration - I didn't even *like* Matt all that much. Still, the words stung as I realized I'd been right after all. He wasn't dating me because of who I was. He was dating me because he saw me as the bottom of the barrel, and he knew he'd have no competition, because who else in their right mind would possibly want me?

I'm happy to say I ended the relationship the very next day. But whatever sense of satisfaction I felt in kicking that asshole to the curb (and thus proving him wrong by demonstrating that, yes, fat women certainly *will* leave) was dimmed by the pervasive knowledge that I simply wasn't good enough. That as long as I looked the way I did, no decent person would ever want to tarnish themselves by going out with me.

At its core, patriarchy is about control: controlling women, limiting our options, shutting us up, forcing us to give birth against our will, paying us less than what we're worth to keep us economically dependent on men, casting us into the shadows while our male counterparts are pushed into the spotlight, and - of course - viewing our bodies as property. The sense of male entitlement to women and sex is being called into question as of late, with social forces such as the #MeToo movement, but the very fact that we need a movement like this in the first place illustrates how very real and deep-seated this issue is.

David Wong, Executive Editor for the pop-culture website Cracked, wrote an excellent and insightful synopsis[21] on this particular brand of entitlement. In it, he drew on cultural norms in television, movies, comic books, video games, and other forms of media, using them to explain why some men feel they are "owed" a woman, or at least sex. "When the Karate Kid wins the tournament," writes Wong, "his prize is a trophy and Elisabeth Shue. Neo saves the world and is awarded Trinity. Marcy McFly gets his dream girl, the hero in Avatar gets the hottest Na'vi...hell, at the end of An Officer and a Gentleman, Richard Gere walks into the lady's workplace and just carries her out like he's picking up a suit at the dry cleaner."

It's a societal contract, he says, likening it to receiving one's paycheck at the end of the month. And when the contract is broken, it leaves room for a sense of injustice on the part of men who have not been "awarded" their perfect female.

"From birth, we're taught that we're owed a beautiful girl. So it's very frustrating, and I mean frustrating to the point of violence, when we don't get what we're owed. These women, by exercising their own choices, are denying it to us. It's why we go to 'slut' and 'whore' as our default insults - we're not mad that women enjoy sex. We're mad that women are distributing to other people the sex that they owed us."

This sense of entitlement is also why so many men respond to female fatness with outright anger and hostility. In the story, the woman is supposed to look a very specific way for her hero. She's supposed to have an impossibly tiny waist, a curvaceous backside, a thigh gap for days, a generous bosom, long hair, and the requisite "come-hither" look. What happens, then, if she's fat? What happens if she's got a round belly, chunky thighs, and a double chin?

The societal contract Wong speaks of has been broken; the trophy in the hero's story is defective, and he has been slighted - cheated out of the prize he deserves. When women are viewed as props - no more than decorative accents - those of us with bodies that deviate from the societal norm are considered unacceptable.

Out of this notion grows the idea that women have a duty to look good for men - as though we owe it to them to have a flawless face and the dimensions of a Barbie doll. Both men and women buy into this idea: the internet is riddled with tips and tricks on "looking good for your man" and "how to make him want you," as well as commentary from men weighing in on women's appearances. "Why do you wear so much makeup? Don't you know that we men prefer natural faces?" (To which I always delight when some cheeky lady responds with a sarcastically pearl-clutching sentiment along the lines of, "Oh dear, I hadn't realized - thank you so much for making me aware of my dreadful faux pas, and as it is my duty to do with my face and body as the men wish, I shall remove the offending makeup at once!") Similar observations are made, by men, about all aspects of a woman's appearance: her hair (guys like it long), her clothing (be sexy in a natural way, but keep it classy, because sluts aren't marriage material), her body (better do six thousand crunches before that date next weekend to ensure your figure doesn't disappoint), her tattoos, her piercings, even her *shoes.*

Sorry, dudes of the world, but I honestly don't give a damn about the amount of makeup you think I should or shouldn't adorn my face with. Similarly, I don't have time to devote my attention to your feelings about my shoes, tattoos, hair, clothes, or body.

Sadly, however, this wasn't always the case.

- 7 -

The Story of My Body

At the age of twenty, I met a man who I developed an instant infatuation for. His name was Dylan, and he was intelligent, charismatic, funny, and charming. I was so naive then, and I was fascinated with the worldly wisdom he eschewed.

He was happy to start sleeping with me, but he made it perfectly clear that I wasn't his type. He liked skinny girls - and I certainly wasn't one of those. Looking back, I cringe at the situation. I want to reach into the past and grab my twenty-year-old self by the ear and drag her away. But, as I've already mentioned, my self-esteem was critically low, and I wanted whatever I could get from him. I resigned myself to the role of fat sidekick, telling myself it was what I deserved. The way I saw it, I was lucky Dylan was even spending any of his time with me.

Remember the illness I brought up in the previous chapter - the one that left me basically unable to eat? It was around this time that whole debacle began, and like all the doctors, Dylan was excited about my resulting weight loss -

so much so that he told me we could start officially dating, as opposed to just sleeping together, now that I was "taking care of myself" (or, losing weight far too quickly through health factors out of my control, but whatever). So we became a couple, and I felt like it was the best thing that had ever happened to me.

Tired of not being able to feed myself and feeling terrible all the time, I eventually tried a very restrictive meal plan that cut out all sorts of foods, then slowly introduced them back into my diet - sort of a system reset. This seemed to do the trick, and suddenly, I could eat again. And yet...

By then, I sort of didn't *want* to eat again. I mean, I'd lost so much weight! It was wonderful! I looked like a whole different person! Dylan approved of my body! I swore to myself that I'd never get back to where I'd been. I'd never *let myself go* like that again.

≳

Fortunately, I then fell into extreme poverty, which ensured I didn't have to worry about overeating, as there was rarely enough food to go around. Dylan and I had moved to a farmhouse in the countryside, and there we encountered many financial hardships. He badly injured his knee and was unable to walk, and without insurance, he couldn't afford the surgery he needed to fix it. He didn't have a car or a driver's license, and the house was many miles away from the nearest town, let alone a bus stop, making it essentially impossible for him to get to a job. I worked twelve-hour shifts at a dialysis clinic in a town about an hour away, making barely enough to cover rent, utilities, and gas for my commute. There was hardly anything left over for food. During the lowest of the low points, we survived off one dented can of baked beans a day, shared between the two of us.

I hated it. I hated everything about it - except the fact that I shed another thirty pounds due to poverty, which brought my grand weight loss total to one hundred pounds. This made me ecstatic. I couldn't afford new clothes, so I had to use safety pins to keep the baggy garments on my frail body. I got so dizzy at work that I'd have to lie down with my feet up. "Low blood sugar," I'd tell my concerned colleagues, "no big deal." Someone would bring me a granola bar or a piece of fruit, and I'd wolf it down, barely tasting it.

Our financial situation did eventually improve, but Dylan had taken a keen interest in my weight loss. He was utterly terrified I'd gain it back, and the next several years were a constant police state over my body, with him in charge.

Let me pause here to disclose that my relationship with Dylan was a violent one, both physically and emotionally. Not initially, of course - low self-esteem notwithstanding, even *I* would have turned tail and run if I'd seen that darkest side of him early on. He carried a deep well of rage and a desire for control - but, as is common in abusive situations, he kept it to himself until I was in too deep. By the time I caught a glimpse of who he really was, we had moved across the country together, joined our finances, and adopted pets. I was in love with him, despite everything, and I made excuses for his behavior.

I write this disclaimer because - unfortunately - I feel the need to explain why I spent so many years with someone who was so terrible to me.

Isn't that the question everyone asks? "Why didn't you just leave?" The answer is unique to every survivor, and is always very, very complicated, but the important thing to note here is that anyone who has endured an abusive situation for any length of time has her - or his - own reasons for staying, and those are valid as hell and should never be called into question.

This isn't a book about domestic violence, so I will step off my soapbox momentarily. But I do feel it's important to mention that one of the main reasons I stayed was my almost nonexistent sense of self-worth. I've already noted that my self-esteem was tragically low when I met Dylan - and after years of emotional abuse, he'd whittled it away even further. And - not surprisingly, given his misogynistic attitude toward women - one of the most-often used tools in his arsenal of shame and degradation was to criticize my body.

It was a weak point, see - and he knew it. He knew how to hurt me the most. He knew how to get inside my head and poison me from the inside out, turning me against myself.

118

"What's this?" he asked sharply one day, pinching my minimal belly fat between his thumb and forefinger.

"Ow!" I pulled away, indignant and embarrassed. I'd gained a few pounds and had been living in fear of him noticing.

"Well?" he demanded. "What is it?"

"My stomach," I mumbled, looking at the floor.

"It's fat," he corrected. "Fat! Why are you getting fat again?"

"I'm not!" My cheeks burned, and I struggled to fight back tears. "I've just had a stressful few weeks - I've been too busy to work out, and I haven't been eating as much healthy food..."

He cut me off. "Always blaming someone or something else. When are you going to grow up and take accountability for your actions? You know how I feel about fat chicks - you've known since we met!"

I was crying now. "I'm *not fat*."

"Not yet. But we all know how capable you are of getting to that point." He sighed, exasperated. "Look - from here on out, I'm going to tell you *when* you can eat and *what* you can eat. And I'm going to tell you when to get your ass to the goddamn gym, because apparently you can't fucking handle it yourself."

I knelt on the floor, head in my hands, sobbing. The shame was *unbearable*. I wanted to vomit, to reach inside myself and pull out all the offending tissue, to surgically remove all the parts of me that were inadequate.

"Get up!" he screamed. "Get off your ass and go to the gym! I don't want to see you back here until you physically can't work out anymore, do you understand me?"

Oh, how my heart aches, writing these words.

His happiness level in our relationship was inversely proportionate to my dress size. At the thinnest point in my adult life, achieved via a thousand-calorie-per-day diet and daily workouts that left me feeling so shaky and lightheaded I could barely trudge back home, I had a job waiting tables in a high-end steakhouse, where the required uniform was a miniskirt and high heels. (For the women, anyway - the men got to wear regular old slacks and shoes, and none of *them* ever collapsed in tears on the locker room floor after an eight-hour shift because their feet were raw and bloody...but that's a feminist rage for another day.) Dylan *loved* my outfit - the little skirt especially - and he'd constantly tell me how sexy I looked in it. Sometimes we'd go out with my coworkers after a shift, and he'd ogle me, staring at my breasts and grabbing my butt in front of everyone.

"Isn't she sexy?" he asked a mutual male friend once. "Doesn't she have a great little ass?" The friend and I were both visibly uncomfortable, but Dylan either didn't notice or didn't care.

We didn't have much money, but occasionally he'd suggest a shopping trip. This always thrilled me to my marrow - until we got to the store, that is, and I realized I was meant to try on the skimpiest little dresses in the shop and parade around in front of him like a prize hog. I never told him how uncomfortable this made me - I didn't allow myself to fully feel the discomfort, if I am being honest. There was an undercurrent of exhilaration to the whole thing - it was lovely to feel desired, despite the objectification that came along with it, especially for a former fatty like myself. I tried to attribute my unease to shyness, plain and simple. I mean, here was someone who wanted to celebrate me for the way my body looked, instead of vilify me for it! That had to count for something…right?

(The correct answer is, NO, it doesn't have to count for *anything*, because all that matters is whether or not I was comfortable, and I was not - but though I understand this now, I didn't then.)

As time went on, this objectification intensified. Dylan began pressuring me into sexual situations that I wasn't down with. Much of the time, these took a lot of convincing - convincing that ultimately became coercion. Always, I had an immediate gut reaction, something akin to revulsion, but if I expressed this openly, he'd bemoan my prudishness and berate me for being uptight and unadventurous. It was easier to just go along with whatever he wanted - not to mention safer, as provoking his temper could be as dangerous as poking a sleeping bear in a cave. Eventually, I got really good at talking myself into things. I'd convince myself that this was what *I* wanted, too. Of *course* I wanted to put on a slutty schoolgirl outfit, complete with the requisite infantilizing pigtails, and try to pick up random men in bars because it was something he got off on observing. Of *course* I wanted to have threesomes with him and his friends so he could show them all how sexy and awesome his girlfriend was. I mean, what girl *doesn't?*

Deep down, I knew I didn't really want these things - knew that the roiling in my gut was shame and disgust, not excitement and anticipation - but I silenced that intuitive voice. Why? Because he never honored my feelings anyway. Because he'd shame me and call me a boring bitch if I resisted. Because maybe he was right and I *was* a boring bitch.

But the number one reason?

Because I believed that *being physically desired* was the be-all end-all - the holy grail. Because, like all of us, I'd been taught from childhood that being a woman meant, in part, being sexualized and objectified, and that these things should be taken as compliments, rather than predations. Because, like most women out there, I'd been socialized to believe that *my feelings, values, and opinions were less important than the satisfaction of the men around me.*

The concept of desirability, and the exercising of it, became a traumatic experience for me. I won't go into the sordid details, but suffice it to say that I, on many occasions, compromised my integrity, my values, and my safety at the request (and, eventually, the insistence) of my partner - because as a woman, I believed this was what was expected of me.

This ball of yarn has taken *years* of therapy to untangle - and it's not finished yet, nor am I convinced it will ever entirely be. I've made a lot of headway, fortunately. I now know that this coercion was sexual abuse; I truly didn't understand that at the time.

Once, when Dylan wanted to have sex, I told him I wasn't in the mood. "Shut the fuck up," he growled, then held me down and did it anyway. I knew better than to struggle; I just hid my face in the blanket so he wouldn't know I was crying.

I was thirty-one years old before I understood that this was *rape*.

I was his trophy, you see. His prize. I owed him. He and I *both* knew it.

It is for reasons like the ones illustrated above that I believe I never felt truly comfortable - truly safe - in my thin body. As long as I was thin, after all, I was desirable - and if men desired me, and insisted on carrying out those desires, I believed I had no choice but to comply.

Fuck the fucking patriarchy and all the harm it causes girls and women every goddamn day. I know this is a book about bodies, not misogyny, but let's be honest - the two are so very often intricately entwined. The abhorrence of fatness, after all, could never exist on such a grand scale if it weren't for misogynistic cultural ideals of the way a woman should look. The toxic notions of desirability and gender roles that we are all taught from a young age are deeply rooted in sexism, misogyny and the patriarchy as a whole, and they're fucking us over in massive ways.

Perhaps unsurprisingly, after several years of keeping up the thin charade, I began gaining weight again. I'd sworn I wouldn't - vowed on everything I held dear that now that I'd achieved thinness, I'd never do anything so stupid as to relinquish it. But years of stress, trauma, gaslighting, and abuse had me feeling like my mind was unraveling, and when I began disappearing into food again as an escape, I filed it under the category of self-sabotage. Furthermore, I used it as a reason to justify my already pervasive belief that I was inadequate - that everything I touched turned to shit eventually, because I was simply lacking as a human being.

But was it really self-sabotage? Looking back, I think not. I think it was self-*preservation*. While it was true that I didn't *actively* want to grow larger, I'd developed a subconscious belief that fatness offered protection - like a suit of armor that's clunky and awkward and not at all convenient to wear, but you know it will at least protect you from the flying arrows.

This certainly wasn't something I consciously conceptualized, but by gaining weight, I was putting up a wall of protection around myself. I was making sure men would no longer find me desirable and would, therefore, stop hurting me.

"Why?" Dylan often demanded answers, believing I owed him an explanation for my slowly growing body. "Why are you doing this to yourself? Why are you doing this to *me?"* There was no reasoning with him. Once, I attempted to explain the concept of stress-eating to him, and he scoffed and said, "What could you *possibly* have to be so stressed about?" As though my life was all sunshine and roses, and I was nothing but a spoiled brat.

I weighed myself multiple times every day - I'd been doing this for years - and I was horrified to see the number creep up, bit by bit, over the months. I lived in fear of Dylan finding out how much I'd gained, and one day, this fear was realized when he summoned me into the bathroom and ordered me to step on the scale in front of him.

I'll never forget the sense of dread, rising in my gut like vomit, and the pounding of my heart. I felt like a caged animal - I wanted to run, to hide, to claw my way out, to do anything to escape. My cheeks burned; my scalp prickled with sweat and fear. With shame and self-hatred roiling through me, I obliged and watched as the dial came to rest.

"One hundred and thirty-four pounds?" he thundered. "One hundred and thirty-four!" The way he was carrying on, you would have thought I'd murdered someone and hid the body under our living room couch.

"*This* is why I can't marry you!" he screamed - he often liked to detail all the ways in which I fell short and was therefore not marriage material. "Because I refuse to have a *fat fucking wife!"*

The words hung in the air, surrounded by an eerie silence, and in that vacuum of sound, one thing became suddenly, explicitly clear.

You are a terrible human being.
I didn't say it. But I thought it.

I don't remember exactly how long it was after that when I finally managed to leave. Too long, that's for sure - at least another year of strict dieting and food shaming still stood between me and escape. Whenever we'd sit down to eat, Dylan would frown at my portion if he saw I'd served myself as much food as I'd served him. I always made sure *never* to finish everything on my plate - at least, not in front of him. Instead, I'd take the dishes to the kitchen to clean up, then wolf down the rest of my food on the way to the sink, when his back was turned.

If he was watching, of course, I wouldn't finish my meal. Then, hungry and depressed, I'd stop at Taco Bell on my way to work in the evenings and inhale a whirlwind of junk food - anything to fill the void. Anything to soothe the ache of simply existing. Ground beef swimming in grease? Bring it on. Neon-hued nacho cheese? The more, the merrier. Scoop after scoop of sour cream? Yes, please. I was miserable anyway, so why not just eat things that tasted good?

I'm happy to report that my life got *so much better* shortly after that, when I finally left Dylan and moved back to my hometown to start my life over again. By then I was in the last year of my twenties, and though I felt relief at my newfound freedom, I was also traumatized and terrified - a deer in headlights, watching the future rush toward me with no idea how I was going to handle it. I was diagnosed with post-traumatic stress disorder as a result of the years of physical, sexual and emotional abuse, and I embarked on a quest to work through it all: to heal, to find myself beneath all those complicated layers of trauma, and to eventually thrive.

During this journey, I was surprised to discover that of all the emotional wounds Dylan had bestowed upon me, one of the most pervasive was the cavernous pit of shame about my body. In fact, it was worse than ever. After leaving him, my weight gain had continued steadily, and I'd put on a large amount of extra pounds in a short amount of time. I kept having to buy new clothes; jeans I'd purchased just a month previously would suddenly be so tight I could barely breathe while wearing them. I'd tell myself I wouldn't buy larger sizes - instead, I'd lose the weight so I could wear the clothes I already had - but after weeks of waistbands digging angry red lines into my hips, I always had to give in. Clothing that caused physical pain served as nothing but a reminder of how bulky, how cumbersome, how *wrong* my body was.

I began draping myself in big, baggy things to hide beneath - and that's exactly what I was doing. I was hiding. I sometimes felt a secret sense of relief at no longer being a target of men's affection. On the contrary - men would glance at me and quickly look away, as though the mere sight of me had the potential to scar their retinas! I was invisible to the male populace - a welcome change from the constant scrutiny of Dylan's critical gaze and the objectification I'd lived with for nearly a decade.

After a year of being single, however, I was feeling ready, albeit tentatively, to re-enter the world of dating - a world I hadn't visited in a decade. I realized, with horror, that I'd be hard pressed to find anyone who could stand the sight of me. I'd been so glad to be invisible to men just a few months earlier; now, I felt chagrined, short-sighted, and stupid.

So I did what I'd always done: I starved myself for a week, then snapped and ate every damn thing in my kitchen, sobbing all the while.

And that's when I started to wonder if I could ever be free from that terrible, soulless cycle. It was around then that I started talking to myself in the mirror. I *had* to. I was dating while in possession of a fat body, which is an act of resistance in and of itself.

You see, I'd wasted enough of my precious time on this earth feeling inadequate and putting myself and my dreams on the back burner. The entirety of my twenties had been spent that way, and I didn't want to do it anymore. I wanted to start a blog, start a business, write books, follow my creative spirit...and I didn't want to wait any longer. I didn't want to postpone my goals for an arbitrary point in time at which I would be thin and, therefore, worthy of such lofty dreams. *Fuck that shit.* I didn't have time for "I'll do it when I've lost fifty pounds" - I wanted it *now.*

But in order to do that - in order to shift my patterns and stop my own body hatred from undermining me at every turn - I had to make a change.

I had to entertain the idea that maybe…just maybe…*it was okay for me to be fat.*

Whaaaaaaat? (Insert the sound of my brain exploding here.)

I struggled with this concept. *Hard.* For a while, I confused *acceptance* with *acquiescence* - as though I would be sacrificing something or giving up on myself. I wondered if this was just a trick my mind had come up with to enable me to be lazy, eat all the ice cream and tacos I wanted, and never set foot in a gym again. I wondered how I could ever embrace the idea that it *was* okay to be fat, when every bit of information I'd ever received on the subject screamed that it definitely was *not.*

It wasn't until I discovered the missing ingredient that I was able to stop hating my body, start actually taking care of it, and finally understand that my worth as a human had nothing (literally *not a damn thing*) to do with the number on the scale.

The missing ingredient?

Self-love.

- 8 -

The Self-Love Revolution

I brought home a book about self-love once. It was called *Madly In Love With Me: The Daring Adventure of Becoming Your Own Best Friend,* by Christine Arylo, and the cover had caught my eye. It sounded so nice. Becoming my own best friend? I didn't have many friends at all at the time, and I reckoned I could use one. Additionally, I knew my self-esteem left a lot to be desired; I'd known this since learning about self-esteem in school in my early adolescence and recognizing, on a visceral level, that it was something I didn't have much of. I didn't know how I knew, but I just *knew* - and that hunch was correct. Perhaps this book could help me address my wounded self-esteem, I thought.

I was *so* excited to show the book to Dylan. He was always happy to see me reading books that would make me a better person, in lieu of "time wasters." Once, he'd caught me reading the latest novel by one of my favorite authors, and it was as though I'd committed a felony. "All this work you have to do on yourself, and you throw away your time reading fiction? *Fiction!"* He was roaringly angry over it, and from then on, I made sure to only let him see me reading things that fell under the category of self-improvement.

(For the record, I didn't ever *stop* reading fiction. In fact, it became my own private rebellion. I did it during the rare moments that he wasn't at home with me, digging out novels I'd stashed in between stacks of out-of-season clothing and behind the cleaning supplies under the bathroom sink - places I knew he'd never look. Fiction books were my escape. For a few moments, I could lose myself in the pages of someone else's life and forget about my own. But this was a luxury I had to steal for myself, so as far as he was concerned, I'd given up fiction entirely in favor of books that would make me smarter, thinner, more obedient, more motivated, or a better girlfriend.)

"Look what I found!" I told him, thrusting the self-love book at him proudly. He read the title, did a double-take, read it again...and burst out laughing.

"Are you fucking kidding me?" he asked, barely able to contain his mirth. "This is a load of garbage. Look, I'll tell you how to love yourself: be *worthy* of your own love. See? It's simple!" He tossed the book across the room. "All this self-love shit does is give people excuses not to work on themselves. And the last thing you need is a book like that. You need to do the work first - and once you're the person you want to be, *then* you get to love yourself."

With my cheeks burning, I looked at the book, lying in an awkward position on the floor where it had landed. "I just thought maybe I could work on my self-esteem," I said sheepishly, apologetically.

Dylan rolled his eyes, clearly exasperated at my stupidity. "Know why your self-esteem sucks?" He continued without waiting for a response. "It's because you're doing a shitty job at life! Just do a better job - *voila!* Your self esteem will be fixed, because for the first time in your fucking life, you'll actually be worthy of it - and you won't need some lame-ass *girl power* book to do it." His lips twisted cruelly around the words *girl power*, the way they always did - he regularly used the phrase to show his disdain for the silly idea of women trying to empower themselves and each other. "Now, go read something that's actually going to make our lives better."

I returned the book the next day, feeling stupid and childish for ever thinking I could love myself without...well, without changing every single thing about myself first.

I wish I hadn't. I wish I'd read the book anyway - squirrelled it away as though it was one of my beloved fiction books and read it in bits and pieces during the occasional stolen moment. Maybe some of it would have sunk in. Maybe I would have realized a lot sooner just how incorrect Dylan's understanding of self-love really was.

WHAT SELF-LOVE ISN'T

The notion that self-love is conditional - that we don't deserve it until we've done the thing or made the money or lost the weight or fixed the problem or [insert quantifiable goal here] - is highly flawed, extremely toxic, and actually *counterproductive* to growth and success. Yet so many people out there seem to share Dylan's point of view: that we only get to love ourselves when we've crossed everything else off our self-improvement list. This, more than anything else, displays a fundamental cultural misunderstanding of the concept of self-love.

Due to social conditioning, we've packed a whole load of nonsense into these two little words and the hyphen that connects them. As we've already examined, none of us are immune to this conditioning; it's a byproduct of existing within a society. The good news? Just as we've *learned* these behaviors and belief systems, so too can we *unlearn* them!

In order to start the unraveling, let us first put together a list of common myths about self-love, so we can identity what it *isn't*.

Myth #1: Self-Love Is Selfish

Our culture is unashamedly obsessed not only with Doing All The Things, but doing them perfectly. This is reflected in social media feeds worldwide; everyone's posting only the prettiest and most admirable parts of their lives. Never mind that 90% of our home looks like the aftermath of a violent natural disaster; what we'll post on Instagram is the three square feet of clean space in the entire house, decorated with a small plant and a coffee mug emblazoned with a cheeky quote so that the world will know how easy and breezy and beautiful and *fun* our lives are.

If you're a parent, you have to be the *best* parent: start your kid on piano lessons at age 3, teach them a second language before kindergarten, ensure they consume only home-cooked organic/free-range/gluten-and-soy-free/plant-based diets, volunteer in their classrooms, facilitate summers in Europe for the purposes of cultural immersion, and arrange weekend play dates that would make Martha Stewart proud. Of course, hardly anyone actually has the time, energy, or resources to carry all this out. Still, we run ourselves ragged trying - and when we simply *can't do any more* because we need to sleep or take care of ourselves, we're made to feel guilty. As though we're somehow shortchanging our children by not completely abandoning our own needs and giving every aspect of our lives over to them.

If you're an entrepreneur, you have to be the *best* entrepreneur: work seventeen-hour days, never take a day off, create a flawless email newsletter/website/brand strategy/launch party/marketing campaign, and make $50k in your first month of business - and if you don't, you're *doing it wrong.*

If you're working your way up the career ladder, you have to put in sixty-hour work weeks, be on call at all hours of the day, be expected to miss family dinners/children's birthday parties/sisters' weddings if something comes up at the office, and answer five a.m. text messages from your boss. Otherwise, you obviously don't want the promotion enough.

Where, in all of this madness, does self-love fit in? The answer is: it doesn't. If we want to cultivate it in our lives, we have to make time for it. We have to make *room* for it.

But, as our culture constantly reminds us, making room for something as frivolous as self-love is horribly, appallingly *selfish*.

Right?

Wrong.

We've all heard the phrase "you can't pour from an empty cup" - but most of us act as though it somehow doesn't apply to us. Take my word for it: *it applies*. To you, to her, to him, to every damn one of us. If we aren't taking the time to love and appreciate ourselves as we are, we're incapable of giving fully - to our kids, our clients, our employers, our friends and family, and the world. I'll explain *why* this is true in just a few pages. For now, I ask for your trust that it is.

Looked at from this point of view, it's clear that self-love is about as *un*selfish a thing that ever existed - because self-love facilitates better opportunities for more honest, energetic, and genuine self*less*ness.

Myth #2: Self-Love Enables Laziness & Inaction

This was Dylan's primary belief about self-love - that if I embraced it, I'd see fit to stop learning, growing, or trying at anything, for the rest of time.

I guess it sort of makes sense. If you think you're great, I can understand how some people would assume you'd be content to stay exactly as you are for the remainder of your days on this earth.

Realistically, though, that is not how it goes.

Think of a task that's been weighing on your mind for some time. For me, it's always something related to cleaning or organization: getting rid of all the clothes in my closet that I haven't worn in years, or finally wading through the pit of paperwork in my office that's needed filing since 2009.

Picture that task, and then imagine trying to tackle it on a day when you feel like complete shit about yourself. You know the days I'm talking about: the ones in which you'd rather hide in bed all day than face yourself in the mirror. Think about a day like that, when you're stewing in self-hatred, and think about opening that closet door and looking at the mess - a colossal, gargantuan, what-fresh-hell-is-this mess - and feeling *any* sort of desire, drive, or motivation to get it done.

On the flip side, what if you woke up one morning feeling *great* about yourself? What if you opened your eyes and fully believed, beyond a shadow of a doubt, that you were strong, capable, beautiful, smart as hell, and ready for whatever came your way? What would happen if you flung open the closet doors in that state of mind? Most likely, you'd find it a lot easier to roll up your sleeves, dive in, and get cleaning.

Maybe you're one of those magical people who use self-loathing as a tool to help you pop out of bed and start gaily crossing items off your to-do list - but if you are, you're in the minority, my friend. For the vast majority of us, attempting to achieve something like this when we're feeling like complete shit about ourselves is, frankly, as ridiculous as the average Joe deciding one day to climb Mount Everest without the proper training and conditioning. It's an insurmountable obstacle.

Self-*love* doesn't keep us from doing things - self-*hatred* does. We see it all the time: we stay in careers we can't stand, justifying our actions by insisting "I'd never find anything else that paid me enough." We hang on to relationships and situations that aren't serving us because we're afraid we won't be able to find anything better. We ignore our dreams of learning to play the bassoon or running a marathon because we're scared we won't be able to do these things well - or at least, not well *enough*. Self-hatred breeds paralyzing fear. Self-love, however, empowers us to feel the fear and *do it anyway*.

As I mentioned previously, I stayed with Dylan for nine years. And for at least five of those years, some part of me understood that it wasn't healthy and I needed to get the hell out of dodge - but my lack of self-love kept me from taking the leap. For *nine years*. If I'd begun practicing self-love earlier in my life, I'd have hightailed it the fuck out of there the first time he hit me - probably even before, when the red flags started popping up like a game of Whack-A-Mole. But because my self-love tank was perpetually running on empty, I stayed in a dangerous situation for *years* longer than I should have. At the time, leaving that relationship was my messy-ass closet. It was the insurmountable task - the thing I knew I needed to do, but couldn't fathom how I would actually pull it off. At my lowest of low points, successfully escaping that relationship seemed as much of an impossibility as sprouting a pair of wings and flying away.

I had no love for myself, you see - which meant I also had no confidence and no faith in my ability to turn things around.

These things are intricately interwoven. Confidence without self-love is mere bravado. There's nothing behind it - nothing to back it up.

In other words, we can *tell* ourselves we're going to clean out that closet until we're blue in the face, but until we're operating from a place of self love, we're probably not going to believe we can actually get it done.

Myth #3: Self-Love Is Arrogant

Think of the most arrogant person you know. Not gonna lie: the one who comes to mind for me is none other than Donald Trump.

Donald Trump thinks he's the shit, right? He thinks he's a genius. He thinks he should be worshiped and revered for - well, presumably, for his leadership abilities, although many of us would disagree. Donald Trump is a man who thinks very, very highly of himself.

But does he *love* himself, in the truest sense of the word? Does he practice active self-love?

Abso-fuckin-lutely not.

I don't know the man personally, but his lack of self-love is obvious. All the singing he does of his own praises

139

isn't coming from a place of true, genuine love for himself, but from a place of arrogance - arrogance that appears to be covering up a giant stinking pit of deep-seated insecurity and, dare I say, *self-hatred*.

Honestly, I doubt he even knows that pit is there. I don't believe he's devoted a single second of his time here on earth to healthy self-reflection and introspection. And he can walk around saying he loves himself all he wants - but nothing will ever, *ever* convince me that's true.

I believe that, if we truly love ourselves, we are incapable of doing, or are at the very least disinclined to do, any of the following:

- Perpetuating discrimination and hatred
- Being categorically dishonest
- Pushing others down to boost ourselves up
- Promoting ideologies or practices that bring harm to others
- Refusing to extend help to those who need it most

My friends, these are not actions and behaviors that are rooted in love; on the contrary! These things smack of arrogance and narcissism, not loving kindness.

On the flip side, someone who operates from a place of authentic self-love will own their accomplishments and victories - but they will not hurt *others* in the process of getting to where they want to be. Loving ourselves fully requires us to act with integrity - to make sure we can *live* with ourselves. By contrast, if we do the things on the list above, we have to *lie* to ourselves in order to live with ourselves. We have to cover our deep-seated hatred with layers of arrogance - otherwise, we'd drown in our own self-created misery.

And that's not self-love. It's the polar opposite. It's dishonest. It's wrong. It's the bravado I spoke of in the previous myth: confidence without self-love to back it up.

WHAT SELF-LOVE IS

Now that we know self-love is not selfish, lazy, or arrogant... let's move on to defining what, exactly, it is.

1. Self-Love is Foundational

Here's the secret.

In order to make any lasting, meaningful, and fulfilling changes in our life...self-love always, *always* has to come first.

Why would we do something, after all, if we don't believe we deserve it? Even if we truly want it - even if we know, deep in our hearts, that it's the thing that lights us up - if we don't understand that we are *already* deserving of it, we won't get very far.

Have you ever known someone who wrapped their identity up in their successes and accomplishments? Perhaps you do this yourself; many of us do. It's not uncommon for someone to find success and experience an increase in self-esteem because of it. And taken at face value, that's not necessarily a bad thing - until it becomes clear that this person's entire identity rests on their success and accolades. Success is the foundation that they've built their self-esteem upon.

Pro-tip: foundations should be unshakeable. That's kind of the *point*. And success? That's not unshakeable.

Neither is money, or a relationship, or a job, or a title, or a big house, or a fancy car. Anything can happen at any time. As you read this, we're literally hurtling through space on a massive rock at an incredible rate of speed. *Everything* is a risk. Being alive is a risk, in and of itself.

If your identity - your foundation - is built on your net worth, for example...what happens when the stock market crashes and all those shares you own are suddenly worth next to nothing? What happens to your sense of self when the very foundation it's built upon crumbles to dust?

What if we build our identities around the people we're romantically involved with? If we only know ourselves in relation to our significant others, the ending of the relationship can have disastrous effects on our sense of self. Worse yet, we may not even have a sense of self to *begin* with if we see ourselves merely as extensions of our partners. Breakups are hard even for the healthiest and most well-adjusted couple - but for a person without his or her own identity, it's a meltdown waiting to happen.

Companies can go under, jobs can be lost, weight can be gained, relationships can be ended, houses can be foreclosed upon, cars can be repossessed, and bank accounts can be emptied. *Nothing* is permanent. And when the unthinkable happens - when we lose everything - what we're left with is, quite literally, all we have.

Ask yourself this question: if you lost everything...what would you have?

This is why self-love as a foundational practice is so important. When you build the structure of your life on a solid slab of self-love, a wall can fall down or the roof can collapse, but you will always, *always* have your most important resource: yourself. Self-love fosters resiliency in the face of strife. It gives us the boost we need to keep going, even when everything has gone to hell in a handbasket. It reminds us that we can get through this, because we're strong and awesome and so very much *enough* - and we don't need money or supermodel bods or fancy titles to believe in our own badassery.

2. Self-Love Frees Us From Comparison

When we show up for ourselves with love, we get to call the shots. We get to decide what we want out of life - and we're no longer stuck looking to cultural and societal standards for success, then beating ourselves up when we can't quite fit the mold.

Comparison is a killer - of confidence, motivation, and dreams. It's all too easy to fall prey to it in this day and age, when everything's got to be Instagram-worthy or it doesn't count - but we don't *need* to live our lives constantly monitoring how we measure up to others.

Have you ever had one of those days where you feel really beautiful? Maybe your hairstyle is on point or your clothes fit just right or your eyes seem especially blue and sparkly. You walk around on cloud nine for a while - and then, you see her: the sexiest, most gorgeous specimen of feminine beauty ever to exist. Suddenly, your own confidence begins to plummet. Never mind the fact that *your* appearance hasn't actually changed at all; you *feel* as though it has. You feel like the ugly duckling in the room - and comparison is the culprit.

Our society likes numbers and labels and neatly quantifiable things. Knowing where we are in relation to others is comfortable; it gives us an idea of where we fit in the structure of things. All too often, however, we fail to recognize that this structure is an altogether human creation. Do flowers compare themselves to one another? No - they just bloom. Does the river wonder how it measures up to all the other rivers? No - it just flows. Does the mountain deem itself better or worse than the peaks around it? No - it just stands tall. In the same way, self-love is the act of letting go of that comparison. It's the act of allowing ourselves to bloom, flow, and stand tall, regardless of what the people around us are doing, or saying, or thinking. Then, and only then, can we approach life from a place of true, genuine authenticity.

When we compare ourselves to others, we limit our own growth. We hone in on the negative, because that's what our brains are wired to do - and our creativity, motivation, and inspiration goes down in flames. However, when we give up the comparison game and choose instead to show up in authenticity, we can trust ourselves to evaluate our current position, others' opinions be damned. We know that as long as we *feel* good about what we're doing or how we look or who we are, that's all that matters. Everything else is just noise.

3. Self-Love is Unconditional

There are no strings attached to it; it can't be taken away from you. Not even if you lose your ass in the stock market and end up living in a cardboard box. Let's hope it doesn't come to that - but it's a valuable question to ask ourselves. Would you still love yourself if that cardboard box and the clothes on your back were your sole possessions?

I would. And I believe everyone should. Because self-love doesn't come with conditions.

Dylan would beg to differ. He believed that I didn't deserve to love myself until I'd kept the house perfectly clean for six months straight, never let leftovers go bad in the fridge, fit into my size zero jeans again, patched up the yawning pit of need within his soul, and invented the cure for cancer. Not that he ever said the last two, as such, but it became pretty obvious over the years that nothing I did would ever be good enough. As soon as I'd met one milestone, he'd have another ready and waiting - more hoops to jump through before I'd won the grand prize of being worthy of my *own* love and respect and, therefore, his.

It doesn't take an abusive partner, however, to put this belief system into play. All too often, we do it to *ourselves*. I know I have.

Just as we can't base our self-love on material things, we also can't base it on a set of conditions - and here's why.

Let's say we are, like so many others, using weight loss as our self-love barometer. Let's say we believe we'll be deserving of our own love when, and only when, we lose 30 pounds. We'll put in extra time at the gym. We'll restrict the hell out of our food options. We'll devote our energy and focus to losing the weight - and, let's say we do it! Let's say we're now 30 pounds lighter, ready to soak up all that self-love.

Our body has changed - but our *mind* hasn't. We're still the same people we were before we lost the weight - and we *feel* the same. Sure, those pesky 30 pounds are gone, but the cellulite is still there. So are those stretch marks on our stomach and the flab on our thighs. We notice these things in the mirror and experience a sinking feeling - because we're realizing we *don't* deserve our own love. Not yet. Not until we do more. Get thinner. Look better. Those women in the lingerie ads - we need to look like *they* do! *Then*, we can love ourselves...

And so the cycle continues. With each milestone, we expect massive internal change - change that never comes, because external shifts alone won't affect our internal landscape. And because we don't *feel* any different when we hit our milestone, we take it to mean, consciously or unconsciously, that we don't deserve the self-love *yet*. We don't get to relax into ourselves yet, because we're not quite where we want to be.

What we're actually saying to ourselves throughout this cycle is that *we don't believe we will ever deserve our own love as long as we remain who we are*. And that's really, really sad.

Spoiler alert: we're *never* going to be exactly where we want to be, because those things we imagine in our heads are just that - imaginary. Real life rarely, if ever, lives up to those ideals. So what are we doing, placing our self-love on hold and lying in wait for the pretty pictures in our heads to come to fruition? It's nuts.

Instead, we need to focus on developing our self-love muscles *first* - and trust that everything will fall into place from there.

As you can see, the notion that self-love is something we have to earn is entirely flawed. We don't need to achieve a certain set of milestones in order to be deserving of our own love. Instead, we need to love ourselves, fiercely and without shame, in order to make our way through the world with confidence, grace, and authenticity.

If we all went through our days basking in the glow of unconditional love for ourselves, after all...what a gentler, kinder world we'd live in.

We'd be nicer to others and stop saying mean things about ourselves. We'd go out and chase our dreams - and we wouldn't let a few negative opinions dissuade us from our belief that we could make magical things happen. We'd stop spending time lamenting our reflections in the mirror and instead use that time to actually *live our lives*...all because we'd made the choice to hop on the self-love train.

Love yourself first, and everything else will come into alignment.

- 9 -
Love Thyself: A How-To Guide

In this chapter, I'll be offering a plethora of exercises, activities, and rituals you can introduce into your life to heighten your sense of self-love as it pertains to your body.

There's no one-size-fits-all approach to loving and respecting our bodies in thought and action. Some of these exercises may seem ridiculous, or even terrifying. They may be so far out of your comfort zone that there's no way you could ever see yourself doing them.

That's okay.

You know yourself better than anyone. If these exercises feel too intense to you - if they threaten your emotional safety - you have full permission to skip them.

However, before passing something up, take a moment to pause and ask yourself *why* you don't want to do it. Sit for a moment in silence and let your inner wisdom guide you. Chances are, you *can* do the hard things - even in the face of fear. If you're hesitant to participate in any of these exercises because they seem too difficult or would require you to be too vulnerable, it's important to note that this is your fear talking. And moving forward through fear - that is, feeling the fear and doing it anyway - is a great way to flex your empowerment muscle and build trust with yourself that *you've got this.*

Exercise 1:

GET GROUNDED

We spend our lives moving through the world in our bodies; yet, we are so rarely *in* our bodies with our full attention. Women especially tend to detach from our bodies, living life entirely in our heads and feeling little connection to our physical form.

We do this because we are taught, from early ages, that our bodies - especially the parts below our waists - are shameful. Some of us are told this outright; others are not, but we absorb the message from our prudish and misogynistic society. *Yes, you have a vagina - but you must never speak of it, touch it, share it with others, or think of it as anything other than a medically necessary vehicle through which you will please your future husband and someday reproduce.* This attitude is so pervasive that many girls and women have come to accept it as a fact of life, rather than an antiquated idea that can - and should - be fought back against.

Think of the "period handoff" - you know the one. Aunt Flo's come a day early and you're not prepared, so you have to borrow a tampon or pad off your classmate or co-worker. You whisper in her ear that you need one, she rifles furtively through her bag, and you two do a secretive, sleight-of-hand exchange that would mystify even the best CIA operative, as though the tampon is a national secret that must be guarded at all costs. Sound familiar? We go through this song and dance because we as a society have so much shame surrounding the female reproductive system that it's unthinkable to be seen holding a feminine hygiene product - a product that most girls and women will require for several days out of the month, *for forty-odd years of their lives.*

In our culture, vaginas and shame go hand in hand, which is why so many of us with vaginas unconsciously disconnect from them. There are other reasons why we dissociate from our bodies as well:

- Trauma from sexual or physical violence
- Desire to separate from our femininity due to perceiving it as weakness
- Hatred of or dissatisfaction with one's physical body

The good news is that we can counteract this disconnect and learn to fully integrate our physical selves with our emotional selves. We do this through grounding exercises - activities that help us feel more connected to our bodies and present in the physical world around us. When we do this, we become more intimately familiar with our bodies and ourselves, which is an important first step toward adopting a mentality of unconditional self-love.

How To Do It:

Grounding is a form of meditation, and meditation is a highly personal experience. Different methods work for different people. That said, here are a few techniques that work well for me when I notice I'm not very grounded in my body.

The Honey Drip

Sit, stand, or lie in a comfortable position. Take a few deep, cleansing breaths, feeling the cool air travel through your lungs. Picture that air being pulled deep into your belly, filtering through your entire being: arms, legs, hands, and feet. Do this for three or four breaths, or until you feel present and centered.

Next, concentrate on a spot about the size of a coin at the top of your head, right in the center. Picture a slow stream of warm liquid - pure as water, but thick and leisurely as honey - beginning to drip down from that spot, on all sides of your head.

Feel the warmth (or coolness, if that feels more comfortable to you) begin to spread slowly downwards, to your ears, the muscles in your face and jaw, your neck, your shoulders. Really linger on each spot, paying attention to the feelings and "activating" the nerves in each area.

Feel the warmth creep over your shoulder blades and down your spine, over your chest, down your belly, your arms, your hands, your fingertips. Keep breathing deeply, pulling clean air all the way into your stomach.

Feel the warmth slide slowly down over your hips, your buttocks, your genitals, and the fronts and backs of your legs. Feel it descend your thighs, your knees, your calves, your ankles, your feet, entirely encompassing your lower limbs.

The purpose of this exercise is simply to help bring your awareness to the parts of your body that you may not often think about, especially the lower extremities and the back of your butt and legs. The process of letting the warmth drip down over your body should take at least 3 minutes. Remember to keep taking deep belly breaths for the duration of the exercise.

Make Like A Tree

This exercise is best performed standing.

Close your eyes and take a few deep, cleansing belly breaths. Picture your body, from your shoulders to your ankles, like the trunk of a tree: firm, strong, rooted. Concentrate on the power that's centered within your lower extremities - the power that a tree's trunk must have in order to keep it upright.

With your mind's eye, travel downward from your legs to the soles of your feet. Picture roots growing from them, deep down into the ground, a hundred feet below into the dark, quiet, moist soil of our mother earth. See the roots twisting, curling, going deeper and deeper, anchoring you to the ground and integrating you as part of the soil.

Notice the strength this gives to the trunk: your ankles, your shins, your calves, the front and back of your thighs, your buttocks, your hips, your belly, your back, your chest, and your shoulders. Know that a fierce wind could blow, and still you would stand, strong and steady.

Now, bring your awareness above your shoulders, to your neck and head. This is where the trunk of your tree begins to branch and grow leaves. Picture the leaves like a large halo, extending a few feet out from your head in all directions. You may want to imagine that the leaves are all the thoughts that occupy your mind.

Picture a wind blowing through the room and notice what happens to the tree. The leaves flutter and wave. The branches, somewhat flexible, bow and dance in the breeze. The trunk, however, stays strong and solid, ever more so as it approaches the ground, and the roots connecting you to the earth hold fast.

Keep breathing deeply and stand in your power like this for a few minutes, picturing yourself as a tree and experiencing your inviolable connection with the earth below.

The Body Scan

This exercise is designed to help you find and relieve tension in all parts of your body, bringing you back into your self and promoting a sense of well-being and relaxation within your body. It is best performed sitting or lying comfortably.

Taking deep, cleansing breaths, bring your awareness to the top, front, back, and sides of your head. Scan this area for any tension. Do you sense tension or pressure in your temples? Your jaw? Your tongue? The place where your skull meets your neck? Find this tension, and imagine a warm, golden light spreading through it, melting it away. Allow the area in question to fully relax.

Move downwards to your neck. Is there tension in your throat? Your shoulders? Shine the light on it and lovingly release it.

Keep traveling slowly down the length of your body, finding the tension and releasing it. If you're having trouble focusing, it may help to physically clench or tighten the muscles you're focusing on, then release them, picturing the tension melting away as you do so. Take your time, and make sure to pay close attention to the back of your body as well as the front. Keep going down your chest, belly, back, waist, hips, butt, thighs, calves, shins, ankles, feet, and toes.

Alternatively, you can start at the toes and work your way up if this feels more comfortable.

Many people have trouble concentrating during meditation; if this is you, you're not alone, you're not "doing it wrong," and there's nothing wrong with *you*. It's *really hard* to simply sit, stand, or lie in silence, with nothing to occupy our minds but the present moment. Meditation is something you can practice for years and *still* experience difficulty with. It's not easy, nor is it always comfortable - but sitting through the discomfort and doing it anyway has tremendous benefits, physically, mentally, and emotionally.

Some people prefer guided meditations as a way of helping stay more focused. If this sounds like something you'd like to try, guided meditations abound on the internet. I highly recommend the app Insight Timer and use it almost every day in my own meditation practice. At the time of this writing, the app offers over 100 free guided meditations specifically geared toward grounding.

If you're feeling skeptical about how this meditative hocus-pocus can help you love your body - you're not alone! However, if you can set aside your doubt, place your trust in the effectiveness of getting grounded, and spend just a couple minutes each day doing these or similar exercises, you will begin to notice a much deeper level of connection to your physical body - and that's the first step toward loving it.

The Takeaway:
Most of us live our lives in our heads. When we make a point to bring ourselves back into our bodies, we can begin to build better relationships with our physical forms.

Exercise 2:

GET AWARENESS

In order to solve a problem, we first have to understand the scope of it. Until we know what we're dealing with, after all, we can't accurately assess how we're going to fix it.

Loving our bodies is no different. In order to come to a place of unapologetic and unconditional self-love, we must first figure out the specific ways in which we treat ourselves with hatred.

How is this done? By simply *becoming aware* of the toxic things we say to ourselves.

This is an exercise I did many, many times during my journey toward self-love - and one of the most important and effective. Up until I tried it, I had no idea just *how* pervasive my harmful notions about fat and fatness were. Understanding the scope of it helped me identify my major triggers and give myself grace when I slipped up.

Once I began paying attention, I was *shocked* to learn how deep my hatred for my body really ran. The negative thoughts began as soon as I woke up in the morning and didn't cease until I fell asleep at night. I noticed them while taking a shower, getting dressed, doing my makeup, going to work, even talking on the phone and sending emails at the office. I noticed them at the grocery store, the gas station, and the bank. They happened literally *hundreds of times a day*.

If it sounds disheartening - it is! Make no mistake - this exercise, though simple, is difficult to deal with. The sense of sadness I experienced after realizing the full depth of my body hatred was profound - but it also led me to an important discovery: the *nature* of my negative thoughts.

I'd realized, after spending a few days paying attention, that my negative thoughts about my body were concentrated around *a fear of what other people would think of me*. For example, even if I was alone, I'd catch a glimpse of my cellulite in the mirror, and shame would flood my being, accompanied by the thought: "I can't let anyone see this." If I was running errands, I'd constantly obsess about how massive my ass must look to the people around me. I realized that *literally every single time I looked into the eyes of another human being,* I was preoccupied with what they thought about my body.

It was a hard thing to realize. It brought me to tears. But I learned something important: fearing judgment from others was a *major* trigger for me. If I could get rid of that fear, and the accompanying sense of shame...I could significantly reduce my body hatred right along with it.

Another benefit of this practice, aside from identifying the roots of our self-hatred, is the ability to gently and lovingly correct ourselves when we find ourselves having negative thoughts about our bodies. We can't fix something we don't know is happening - but when we're paying attention, we can notice the toxic thought and say to ourselves, "Wait a minute - that's unkind." The more we practice the act of gentle and loving correction, the more automatic it will become.

Full disclosure: I still have the negative thoughts. *All the damn time.* They don't happen nearly as often as they once did, but they're still around. However, now that I'm adept at catching them, I am able to notice them *without believing them.* When I catch the thought, for example, "She probably thinks you look disgusting," I can look at it impartially - *"Hmmm, that's definitely rooted in fear, not reality"* - rather than taking it as truth.

How To Do It:

The exercise requires only that you *pay attention.* All you have to do is notice the negative thoughts about your body that come up throughout the day. That's it. It's both easy and hard - easy because it's simple, and hard because the things that come up are often painful to face. Do it anyway. The information you'll receive will be invaluable in your journey to love yourself just as you are.

In the morning, set the intention to *pay attention.* Then, go about your day as usual. Perhaps you get dressed. As you pull a shirt over your head, you look at yourself in the mirror and wonder if your stomach looks too fat to wear this. *Ding!* There's one: a negative thought about your body.

When you notice the negative thoughts, it's *very important* not to judge yourself for them. All you need to do is *notice* them. Observe them like you're a scientist with a microscope and your thoughts are the cells in the petri dish. Be impartial and objective.

It's unrealistic, of course, to expect yourself to catch every single negative thought you have about your body throughout the day - because, if you're anything like me, they're happening more often than you realize. That's okay. As long as you remember to pay attention as often as possible, you'll still receive valuable information.

Take care to notice, too, if the negative thoughts you have about your body are connected in any way. What are they rooted in? You may become aware of an underlying theme, much like I did when I discovered that most of my negative thoughts were informed by a fear of judgment from others. In this way, you can identify your triggers and become better equipped to counter the negative thoughts, rather than accepting them at face value.

The Takeaway:

We may not ever be able to completely rid our minds of toxic thoughts - but taking the time to notice them gives us room to exercise some control over how they affect us. We get to decide whether or not to listen to what they're telling us - and when we stop believing their validity, we've made massive steps forward in our journey toward self-love.

Exercise 3:

GET GRATEFUL

We've all heard experts sing the praises of gratitude. We've seen all the planners for sale that now include a spot to write down our daily gratitudes. We've heard the physical, emotional, and mental benefits of giving thanks on a regular basis - and many of us do.

That said, how often do you express gratitude for your *body?*

If your knee-jerk reaction to this statement is that you don't *have* anything to be grateful for where your body is concerned...please don't give up on this. Not yet. Gratitude is *such* a powerful tool. What's more, we don't even have to do anything to attain it. It's *already* in our toolbox - we just have to *use* it. When we do, we may find that the effects are literally life-changing...so I believe we owe it to ourselves to give it a fair shot.

To explain why this is so effective, we must examine the human brain - specifically, the neural pathways within it. Neural pathways are created in the brain based on habits and behaviors. Essentially, they're strings of neurons connected by dendrites. When we repeat an action, more and more dendrites are created in the neural pathway for that action, strengthening the connection. This means, of course, that the more we do something, the stronger its neural pathway grows in our brain. What once was a dirt road has become a highway.

When we regularly express gratitude for our bodies, we start to build neural pathways - natural connections between thoughts about our bodies and the act of, and positive feelings that come from, giving thanks. The more we do this, the more well-traveled and defined those pathways grow, until this gratitude becomes an *automatic* act, rather than a deliberate one. This is exactly how habits are formed - and by building habits of gratitude toward our bodies, we will come to treat ourselves with much more love and compassion - *without even having to think about it.*

How cool is that?

How To Do It:

My challenge to you is this: every day, as part of your morning or evening routine, write down three things about your body that you're grateful for. They can be anything. Maybe you like the shape of your hands or the way your fingernails grow or that one cute little freckle. Maybe you have shiny, luxurious hair or a gorgeous smile or great skin.

What if you don't like *any* of these things? What if you're convinced that every part of you is ugly, unacceptable, and unlovable?

Start listing physical processes! Maybe you hate the shape of your nose…but it helps you smell things, doesn't it?

Your heart is pumping! Your lungs are filling with air! That nasty cut on your finger healed, because - *holy shit* - your body is an incredible, self-sustaining, miracle machine! Remember that time you tripped on the curb and almost fell down in front of a crowd of people, but your reflexes kicked in and your muscles tightened in all the right places and you caught yourself, *all without even thinking about it?* That's utterly *remarkable!* Our bodies are truly mind-blowing in the scope of their amazingness.

You have full permission to repeat gratitudes. You also have full permission to write down things like "My liver is working" or "I didn't catch that nasty cold that was going around" or "both of my ears are exactly the same shape" or "this body allowed me to bear children." It doesn't *matter* what it is, as long as it's some kind of gratitude for something that's happening, or has happened, on or in your body.

The Takeaway:
A regular gratitude practice can change your habits and, by extension, *change your life.* Honest.

Exercise 4:

GET RID OF THINGS THAT MAKE YOU FEEL LIKE SHIT

Here's a hard truth.

There is a very, *very* fine line between the things that motivate and inspire us, and the things that make us feel like shit.

The line is so fine, in fact, that sometimes we can't even tell the difference.

Take a quick mental inventory of your social media accounts. How many do you follow that are based around "fitspiration" or diet accountability, or just skinny people showing off their skinny bodies in cute little bikinis on tropical beaches?

Or when you're standing in line at the checkout counter, scoping the magazines, and you see one featuring an impossibly gorgeous woman with a pert little bottom, a thigh gap, and a 22-inch waist? Perhaps the headline says she's sharing her workout regimen in case you want to look like her! Do you impulsively toss it into your cart, thinking, "I *do!* I *do* want to look like her!"

Perhaps there's an actress you love, but every time you watch one of her movies, you struggle to follow the plot because you're too busy wondering how to get a body like hers?

We all like to think ourselves too wise to be swayed by the influences of the mass media, but the reality is that we're not. *None* of us are immune. And all the activities listed above have something in common: they force us into places of comparison. They have us comparing ourselves to someone else and coming up short. *Every damn time.*

That doesn't sound like inspiration to me. It sounds more like emotional torture.

Comparison kills confidence, self-esteem, and self-love. Its very nature places someone or something above another and creates a kind of hierarchy - a hierarchy we believe we must follow in order to be worthy.

Those #fitspiration Instagram accounts? What they're really saying, behind all the motivational quotes about how nothing tastes as good as being thin feels (but look, have they ever *tasted* the risotto at that Italian joint down the road? I'm just saying), is: "Look at this body. It's better than yours, isn't it? You should fix that." It forces us to draw comparisons and - inevitably - find ourselves lacking.

And that feeling of lack wreaks havoc on our sense of self-love.

There is certainly no shortage of "perfect" bodies to look at on the internet, TV, magazines, billboards, and advertising. We *know* what society's depiction of the ideal body is, thank you very much, and we don't need to see it anymore - not if we're focused on loving ourselves just as we are. Instead, we need to see more bodies like *ours*. More realistic bodies - ones that haven't been airbrushed, photoshopped, starved, surgically altered, or exercised into nothing but skin and muscle.

Fortunately, thanks to the internet, we can see these bodies! The number of social media accounts featuring - and celebrating! - plus-size bodies is growing! Bloggers, photographers, body-positive activists, and even some retailers are displaying Instagram feeds full of big, lush, curvy, fat, and sumptuous bodies (as well as trans and gender non-comforming bodies, too)! Even ten years ago, most folks with bodies outside the conventional spectrum didn't have this kind of representation. And while it's nowhere near enough yet, the fact that I can hop on social media sites and quickly find people who resemble me (and on *fashion blogs,* no less, not fat-shaming sites!) still feels nothing short of miraculous.

Because here's what happens when we start seeing bodies like ours represented in the media: those bodies become more and more normalized. We find ourselves looking at them without judgment and simply *seeing* them. *Witnessing* them. And when we can look at bodies that resemble our own and think of them as normal, rather than disgusting, horrifying, or unacceptable...we can begin to heal from society's toxic attitudes toward fat and fatness.

It should come as no surprise, then, that your task is to rid your life of the flat stomachs and #fitspiration, and instead fill it with stretch marks, cellulite, love handles, and double chins.

How To Do It:

Start by finding *allllll* the Instagram accounts you follow that make you feel like shit and hitting that Unfollow button! Fear of missing out can be a big factor here, so just remember that if ditching these accounts leaves a huge, gaping hole in your life, you can always follow them again. Just try it for a couple weeks, and see what a life without all this comparison feels like to you.

Next, follow body-positive accounts instead. You can do this by searching the following hashtags:

#bodypositive
#bodypositivity
#bodyposi
#bigisbeautiful
#beautycomesinallsizes
#celebrateyoursize
#loveyourcurves
#curvyandconfident
#effyourbeautystandards
#biggirlsarebeautiful

Now that your Instagram feed is a celebration of diverse bodies, let's move on to Facebook. Know someone who's always trying some new diet and obsessively posting about it? Facebook has a handy "Unfollow" feature, through which you can remain friends with this person and not have their posts show up on your feed. They'll never know you did it - no feelings are hurt, none's the wiser, and you don't have to feel inadequate every time you see their before and after shots. This is a great way to set a boundary without giving rise to one of those uniquely 21st-century "I can't believe you unfriended me on Facebook" family dramas.

Don't forget to ditch the diet mags, too. What about the old pair of jeans you keep in your drawer because you're determined to fit into them again someday? Get rid of them; they're not serving you. Oh - and that picture of your favorite celeb hanging next to your bathroom mirror to "motivate" you? Take that shit *down*.

What if the things that make you feel awful about yourself aren't things at all, but *people?* We'll discuss this more in the next exercise, but for now, try to accept the fact that it may be time to either set some firm boundaries, or take inventory of who you really need in your life.

The Takeaway:
In a world full of beautiful uniqueness, comparison is pointless, futile, and soul-crushing. You're already *you* - and that's fantastic, in and of itself. You don't need to be anyone else - and anything that makes you feel otherwise has *got* to go.

Exercise 5:

GET SUPPORT (AND SET BOUNDARIES)

When undertaking a self-love journey, it can be tremendously helpful to share your progress with people you trust, thus keeping yourself accountable to your mission of unapologetic self-love when you slip up (and you will).

How to do it:
Select someone whose help you will enlist to remind you to be kind to yourself, should they catch you talking about or treating yourself in a negative or toxic manner - someone you can trust to *gently* call you out when they hear you despairing about the size of your butt. Emphasis on *gently;* this is not boot camp, and that sort of approach ain't gonna cut it when your goal is to shower yourself with love and kindness.

If this person isn't nearby, try setting up a daily or weekly phone call to check in, during which you will update them on the trials and tribulations of a self-loving lifestyle, and they will remind you that you're beautiful, worthy, and utterly awesome, just the way you are.

Even just *telling* people what you're doing - "Hi, how are you? I'm on a journey to love myself and my body with no strings attached!" - will help you find success. The more often you speak it aloud, after all, the more real it becomes, and the more you'll believe in it - and *yourself.*

If you can think of no one in your life who would be supportive of your body-positive endeavors, please don't despair. Know that just because there doesn't happen to be anyone in your circle *yet* who will understand doesn't mean there's no one out there. You're not alone - and thanks to the magic of the interwebs, we're more connected than ever before! Many Facebook pages and groups exist for this purpose: supporting others in their self-love goals and boosting each other up along the way. Simply search for "body positivity" within Facebook to see how many options are out there! I've met some amazing folks doing exactly this; just because we've never met in real life doesn't mean I don't consider them friends. There are people *all across the world,* ready to offer you love and support in your body positivity journey - what are you waiting for?

As your mindset begins to shift, you will find yourself needing to set boundaries. This can be really, really fucking hard. It's one of the biggest demons I've had to tackle yet - and I'm still fighting it, nearly every day. I still have this ingrained notion that setting healthy boundaries out of love and respect for myself somehow makes me a bitch or a ball-breaker.

But here's the thing. These boundaries aren't *about* anyone else. They're about *you.*

Setting boundaries is a fact of life - but that doesn't make it any easier. There will be people in your life who won't understand. You can *count* on that. Some folks will hear you state your boundary, then try to push it aside as though it doesn't really matter. In these moments, it will be tempting to acquiesce - to appease.

Don't do it.

Remember how we talked about being an advocate for yourself, the way you are for people you love dearly? Summon up that Mama Bear mode and make it known, clearly and firmly, that this is a line you will no longer allow to be crossed. It will probably feel terrifying. It will make your palms sweat and your hands shake and your heart race in your chest. All of that is normal. All of that means *you're doing it right.*

If you're anything like me, you won't always succeed at this. Your urge to prioritize the comfort of others over yourself may be so strong that it won't always let you speak up and define your boundaries. Be prepared for this - and when it happens, don't beat yourself up. Instead, remind yourself, gently and lovingly, why you need these boundaries, so you can do a better job of establishing them next time.

It's all about practice, practice, practice. The more you do this, the easier it gets. It's been quite a few years since my former friend told me I couldn't be successful in a musical career if I was fat. I didn't state my boundary that day - but I sure have since then. Now, if anyone I am communicating with makes a disparaging remark about my body, my appearance, or my fatness, I am able to draw the line. I am able to say, "It is unacceptable for you to speak about my body that way." And I am able to let go of any attachment I have toward their comfort, prioritizing my own well-being instead.

And let me tell you…it feels *good*.

Boundaries don't always have to be announced, either. I had a coworker several years ago who was constantly updating me about her weight loss endeavors, despite me never actually asking. It was hugely upsetting for me; every time, I'd find myself beginning to feel inadequate. I wrestled with the situation - I couldn't exactly stop seeing this person, as we worked closely together five days a week. I didn't want to alienate her by asking her to stop, either - I knew she never *intended* to make me feel badly. Eventually, I decided that I would simply change the subject, consistently and purposefully, whenever she began talking about how many pounds she'd gained or lost. In doing so, I gave myself control over a situation that had previously been quite distressing. Unbeknownst to my coworker, I had set a boundary - and she didn't even have to know it was there.

Setting boundaries carries the added perk of culling toxic people from your environment. Often, if you keep establishing and re-establishing a boundary that these people cannot seem to respect, they'll weed themselves out of your garden altogether, making room for connections to grow - connections with people who honor your boundaries.

People who display a lack of respect for other folks' boundaries are basically great big walking red flags. Let them remove themselves from your life - or remove them yourself, if you must. It's hard to do - but not nearly as hard as continuing to compromise your own values and make yourself small so you won't be in anyone else's way.

The takeaway:
There's lots of support out there, even if it doesn't happen to be in your immediate circle. The more support you seek out, the easier it will be to set boundaries and take ownership over who you let in to your life.

Exercise 6:

GET DEEP

Fact: We can't change our limiting belief systems unless we know what they are. One of the most powerful ways I've learned to do this is a Cognitive Behavioral Therapy technique called laddering.

Laddering helps us look below the surface of our automatic thoughts. It allows us to dig deeper and deeper still, until we hit buried treasure: a core belief that has been hiding away, lurking underground and poisoning our thoughts for years (often since childhood). Once we extract this belief - once we bring it above ground and let the full light of the sun bear down on it - it begins to lose its power over us. And that, my friends, is a beautiful thing indeed.

How to do it:
Think back to Exercise #2, in which you began paying attention to all the negative thoughts you had about your body on a regular basis. Those negative thoughts are often supported by underground root systems that we can't even see - root systems that continue to feed and nourish the harmful

179

thoughts. In order to eradicate them, we have to destroy them at the source.

Look back over your list of thoughts, or notice the next one that comes up. When you have a negative thought, let it come, then ask yourself what it would mean if that were true. For each new statement that comes up, keep asking the same question - what it would mean if that were true - until you find yourself face to face with a core limiting belief.

Let's say the thought that came to mind was "I look so fat." Here's an example of how the laddering exercise would look.

Thought: *I look so fat.*

Ask: What if I *did* look really, really fat? What would it mean if that were true?

Answer: People would think I'm disgusting.

Ask: What if people *did* think I was disgusting? What would it mean if that were true?

Answer: No one would want to be around me.

Ask: What *if* no one wanted to be around me? What would it mean if that were true?

Answer: *I'd be alone for the rest of my life.*

There we have it: the core limiting belief system. As you can see, it doesn't actually have to do with fat or fatness at all, but with the *fear of being alone.* Now, we know what we're actually dealing with, and as we work to address this limiting belief, we may find ourselves hating our bodies less and less.

How do you know when you've struck bottom and encountered a core limiting belief? These usually feel very heavy. Final. Hard to even speak aloud in all their doom. If you're not sure whether an answer is the core limiting belief or not, keep asking the question. Trusting your intuition is important with this exercise; generally speaking, if an answer makes you feel terrified, desolate, or desperate - that's your shovel, knocking against buried treasure.

What happens when you discover a core limiting belief? I'm no therapist, but the following things have been instrumental in my own journey toward excavating limiting beliefs and releasing them from my life.

1. Seeking counsel from a mental health professional.

Therapy used to be fairly taboo - the kind of thing you'd never want to admit to anyone else. Fortunately, as our society grows to understand the importance of mental health maintenance, the veil of silence has begun to lift. Nowadays, there are a lot of places in which you can say "My therapist told me that..." and not be looked at askance. I've personally been in therapy for many years - not because I can't cope without it, but because I find that regular check-ins with a mental health professional do wonders for my state of mind. Many health insurance plans cover behavioral health services, as well, so talk to your doctor or insurance provider and see if therapy may be an option for you.

2. Talking to a trusted friend, relative, or significant other.
This stuff is heavy - don't try to carry the burden alone! Enlist someone you know will hold loving and supportive space for you, and ask them if you can vent about a recent discovery. If you just need to spill but don't want advice, feel free to state that, as well: "I need to get this off my chest, but I'm not really looking for solutions yet - can I just vent to you for now?"

3. Journaling.
I can't recommend this enough. It's private, it's inexpensive, and it requires the bare minimum of tools: a writing utensil and a notebook. That's it. Don't worry about form or structure or spelling or grammar - just sit down in front of that notebook and write whatever comes to mind. It might be a jumbled mess. It might be illegible. It might turn into a grocery list. That's the great thing about journaling: since you're the only one who will ever see it, there's literally no wrong way to go about it. It's extraordinarily freeing, especially for recovering perfectionists like myself, and when done from a place of openness and authenticity, it can be highly therapeutic, offering insights that we may struggle to access otherwise.

As with so many of these exercises, laddering requires a lot of vulnerability, and it's important to engage in active self-care as you peel back the layers. If you find yourself feeling too upset or overwhelmed, stop for the day and do something nice for yourself to lift your spirits. Remind yourself that you embark on this journey from a place of love - and remember that the deep places of the mind are only dark until we let the light in.

The takeaway:
The secrets to what's holding us back are so often hidden in plain sight: buried beneath surface-level thoughts that are easier to swallow. If we spend our lives addressing only that which we can readily see, we risk allowing limiting belief systems to take over our internal landscape. Extricating them can be an emotionally painful process - but the positive impact it can have on our lives is well worth the struggle.

Exercise 7:

GET DRESSED

I'll start this exercise by acknowledging the inherent privilege in it. I fully realize that not everyone can afford to go out and buy new clothes. Additionally, depending on where you live, certain clothing choices may not be available to you.

If, however, you are able to invest in clothing that makes you feel good, this is a great way to instill some good old body-lovin' into your everyday life.

Have you ever worn something you just love? Whether it was a prom dress, that perfect pair of jeans, or an old t-shirt that's so soft, it feels like silk against your skin, it is *amazing* to have our bodies clothed in something we adore.

Unfortunately, many people with larger bodies are denied this pleasure for two primary reasons:

1. Lack of accessibility to plus-size clothes (due to availability, cost, or other factors)
2. Self-punishment

We can't, in this book, do much about the first reason, although I will tell you that plus-size retailers are growing in number, and a quick internet search can help you track down companies that will allow you to shop online (such as Torrid, Eloquii, Modcloth and Asos Curve), as well as some plus-size clothing subscription services as well (like Dia&Co and Gwynnie Bee).

And the second reason - punishment? Really?

Yes, really.

Many of us hesitate to buy clothes that fit properly when we're not happy with our current size. Instead, we squeeze into too-tight jeans, telling ourselves we'll buy new clothes when we lose that extra twenty pounds. This, by the way, is a special kind of torture. Have you ever gotten through a long day wearing jeans that are two sizes too small? It *hurts,* you guys. *A lot.* This is how we punish ourselves: *I'm too big, and I refuse to let myself wear something comfortable until my body is a more appropriate size.*

Or, if we do decide to buy new clothes, we select things that are large and baggy, designed to hide our bodies. Unless your personal sense of style reflects this, it's awfully hard to feel beautiful and confident when you're walking around in the fashion world's version of a pair of drapes. Again, this is a form of punishment: *I will hide my body at all costs, because it is unacceptable and unworthy.*

I was in my thirties before I came to the realization that I could - surprise! - buy clothes that *fit.* Not just *sort* of fit, but fit *well* - as though they were made for bodies like mine. Oh, wait - they *were.* No longer was I resigned to the bland plus-size sections in interchangeable department stores, all of whom seemed to believe that larger women *wanted* to wear the same generic and oversized garb without a hint of femininity, sexuality, or tailoring!

Feeling physically comfortable is an amazing benefit of this exercise - but it's not the only one! In my experience, once I began buying clothes that fit my body the way it was, I felt a greater sense of acceptance toward my physical form. Previously, trying to find clothes for my body had felt an awful lot like trying to stuff the sleeping bag back into the tiny little sack it came in (anyone else?), but once I gave myself permission to shop as though I didn't need to change my body, I was able to experience a whole new sense of freedom and - to my surprise - *fun.*

How To Do It:
Browse the websites for the retailers listed above for some inspiration! Take note of the styles that draw you in - and *ignore* the voice in your head that says "sure, the model looks great in that, but *I* could never..."

Pro tip: that voice in your head? It's fear. While it's perfectly normal to feel a sense of apprehension (or, let's be real, sheer terror) at the thought of showing up in the world, refusing to apologize for your body, it's important to remember that fear is so often *not* a reliable measure of the truth. Your fear spins around in your head and ties your stomach up in knots, because what you're really asking it to do in situations like these is to *let you be vulnerable.* And fear *hates* vulnerability. It will go out of its way to avoid it by filling your head with negativity and doubt, in an attempt to keep you in hiding and avoid getting hurt. Back in ancient times, if we were vulnerable, we were literally putting our life, health, and safety at risk. That's not generally the case now - yet our brains are still wired to operate on this outdated paradigm. When you hear that voice come up as you browse clothing options, take it at face value. Remember that it's not speaking the truth; it's just trying to protect you, albeit with an operating system that's *centuries* behind-the-times. This knowledge can help you honor the fear, thank it for trying to keep you safe, *and* lovingly send it packing; you've got some shopping to do!

If there's a plus-size retailer near you, go into the store and try things on. When you're in the dressing room, your mirror image is looking back at you, and you find yourself having negative thoughts about your body (because this is a prime time for them to show up), remember that *you're there with the express purpose of finding clothes to fit your unique shape.* The whole point of this exercise is to get comfortable looking like *you* - not to try to look like anyone else. This got a lot easier for me after lots of time spent browsing plus-size fashion; the curvier, rounder models gave me a more realistic barometer for what my body might reasonably look like in said apparel, thereby allowing me to take in my reflection and say to myself (or sometimes aloud), "Hey! I look *good* in this!" instead of lamenting the fact that I still didn't have the dimensions of a Victoria's Secret model.

If something catches your eye - try it on! It doesn't matter if it doesn't seem like "you"; you may be surprised to find your personal style evolving as you see yourself in a wider variety of items! And don't automatically go for things that are "slimming," either. (I don't know about you, but I've never been able to feel comfortable in anything with a control-top waist, mainly because I enjoy the freedom to do things like sit, eat, and breathe.)

In fact, within the confines of a private dressing room is a *great* place to try breaking the rules (see Exercise 10)! It's safe; no one's watching. Why not pick out a few things you'd never wear, *precisely because you'd never wear them?* Ask yourself *why* you'd never wear them. Is it because you truly don't like them - or because you've been conditioned to believe someone of your particular size or shape simply shouldn't be seen in a minidress or crop top or form-fitting evening gown?

Remember: you don't have to buy the stuff. Just try it on! Even if these outfits never end up leaving the dressing room, giving yourself the freedom to clothe yourself in things that feel fun, daring, rebellious, lighthearted, or sexy is tremendously liberating.

Unfortunately, there aren't as many bargain-priced options available to those of us with plus-size bodies. I wish there were. I wish every single one of us had the option to walk into a store and walk out of it with clothes that made us feel good, without breaking the bank or taking out a second mortgage. My hope is that, as we move toward a more and more inclusive and body-positive culture, these options will grow and expand and eventually become the norm.

The Takeaway:
Your body is beautiful - just the way it is. And you have every right to clothe it in things that make you feel comfortable, free, and damned *gorgeous*. When you stop looking at your body as a problem that needs to be overcome and begin to accept it as-is, you open the doors for a much happier and self-loving experience of getting dressed.

Exercise 8:

GET PROTECTIVE (aka THE BEST FRIEND TEST)

How do you treat someone when you find yourself overcome with feelings of love toward them? What kinds of things do you say and do? How do you express that love? Likely, your interactions with this person come from a place of support - from wanting what's best for them.

Take a moment to picture a person who you love fiercely and wholeheartedly. For the purposes of this visualization, I'll refer to this person as your best friend, but it could be anyone: your spouse, your child, your sibling, or a parent or grandparent.

Imagine that you are watching your best friend in an interaction with someone else. Imagine the other person telling your best friend that she won't succeed at something she wants to do because of the way she looks. Imagine the way she must feel as she is told some aspect of her appearance is so unacceptable that it will surely nullify her talent, abilities, and drive.

If you're anything like me, this will make you angry. It makes me want to march into that scene, use some choice colorful words to explain to the offending person, in no uncertain terms, why he or she is being an asshole, then wrap myself around my friend like a warm, fuzzy blanket and lead her away from the scene, all the while telling her how amazing and beautiful she is and how much she is capable of.

That's our protective instinct - Mama Bear mode. There's a reason, after all, why it's dangerous to approach bear cubs in the forest: because Mama Bear will *fuck you up* for daring to threaten the safety of her babies. That protectiveness manifests in humans, as well, and it's our way of taking care of those we love.

Most of us have probably had a few moments in which that instinct kicked in and we stepped in to try to protect a loved one. Maybe our kid was being bullied, or our sister was in a relationship with someone who didn't treat her well, or our grandfather's health issues were being handled poorly by medical staff. In situations like these, you probably stepped in to protect the person you love. You probably raised hell with the school principal, urged your sister to end her unhealthy relationship, or demanded better treatment for your grandfather. This is what we do when we love someone: we become their advocate.

Now, let me ask you a question.

How often are you your *own* advocate?

This is far trickier, as it's mired in all sorts of societal norms and connotations of selfishness and self-centeredness. We discussed this in the previous chapter: selfishness is considered such an inappropriate thing to be, but honestly, what's so bad about putting yourself first? Obviously, it's important to be considerate of the needs, desires, and feelings of others, but what so many of us - women especially - tend to forget is that *the needs, desires, and feelings of other people do not automatically take precedence over our own.*

Woah, right?

It's taken me so many years to figure this out, and it's still a daily struggle.

Herein lies yet another problem with the patriarchy: it trains girls and women to be supplicant, pliable, willing to bend over backwards to take care of others while entirely neglecting our own well-being. Think about it. How many times have you been in a situation where someone said or did something that was offensive or made you uncomfortable, but you didn't say anything because you didn't want to "make a scene" or "rock the boat" or "be a buzzkill" or "create drama" or any of those other things that women are apparently so good at?

Yeah. Me, too.

The sad truth is that so many of us live our entire lives elevating the comfort of others over our own well-being. We don't stand up for our rights because we don't want to make *other* people uncomfortable. We're taught that one of the most important qualities to possess is politeness - and it's hardly ever accompanied by a qualifier (such as "be polite, unless someone is trying to walk all over you, in which case, raise ten kinds of hell and stick up for yourself, damn it").

Remember that old nursery rhyme that states girls are made up of "sugar and spice and everything nice," while boys are comprised of "snips and snails and puppy dog tails?" Even in the cute little anecdotes we tell our children, it's insinuated that our duty as girls and women is to be sweet, interesting in a vague and non-threatening way, and, above all, *nice*. Meanwhile, it's perfectly okay for the boys to run around being crawly things and dog parts, with zero fucks given as to who may be upset about that?

I know. It's patriarchal bullshit, exemplifying the misogynistic belief that men exist for themselves and women exist for men - and it affects almost every single woman I've ever known.

What if we ditched this flawed notion that being nice is more important than looking out for ourselves, our needs, and our well-being? We are, after all, the single most important person in our own lives. If we didn't have ourselves, we'd quite literally be dead.

Seriously - *fuck* being nice. Be your own advocate, instead. Take care of yourself before you take care of anyone else. That's not selfishness - it's self-preservation.

How To Do It:

We're great at being protective in situations that involve other people. What about when the person who's treating us like shit is…ourself?

Think back to the beginning of this chapter, when I asked you to picture someone you love. Do me a favor and conjure up that person again. Just as before, it can be anyone you love with your whole heart - anyone you would go to great lengths to protect from harm.

Take a moment to really flesh out the details of this person. Focus in on them, as though they're sitting right here next to you. Visualize the flecks of light in their eyes, the creases in their face, the shape their mouth takes when they laugh.

Now, visualize looking into their earnest eyes and saying the following (feel free to substitute these with things you say to yourself).

"You're disgusting."

"You look like a whale."

"No one will ever love you."

"You're unacceptable."

"You don't deserve happiness."

Watch their face fall. See the tears spill from their eyes. Feel their pain. Notice how *shitty* it feels to cause this person you love so much undue hurt.

It's pretty terrible, isn't it? So terrible, in fact, that you probably wouldn't dream of treating anyone that way - especially someone you love so much.

Right?

Right. Yet *so many* of us spend our lives saying these things to *ourselves*, like it's no big deal.

You guys. IT IS A HUGE DEAL.

The way we talk to ourselves mirrors our internal landscape. That subconscious voice becomes our reality. So it stands to reason that if the things we're constantly saying to ourselves are vile, mean, and cruel, it is unlikely we'll *ever* be able to come to a place of true self-love and authentic happiness.

Come back to this exercise whenever you find your inner voice saying hurtful things to you. Allow yourself to embody the Mama Bear and calmly but firmly make it known that *you will no longer tolerate being treated this way* - by yourself, or anyone else.

The Takeaway:

The golden rule of the Best Friend Test? If you wouldn't say it to your best friend...*don't say it to yourself.* Period.

Exercise 9:

GET NAKED

Remember earlier on, when I described taking off my clothes and looking at my body in the mirror?

Here's where I ask you to do the same thing.

I know. It sucks. When you hate your body, the last thing you want to do is study its every lump, bump, roll, nook, and cranny. Which, my friend, is precisely why we should all be doing it.

If you're anything like I used to be, you either avoid looking in the mirror altogether, or look *only* with the purpose of imagining how you'd look if you lost X number of pounds. When you do this exercise, the goal is to take in your body exactly as it is - not as you *wish* it was.

How to do it:
Strip down and stand in front of a mirror - preferably a full-length, if you have one, so that you're not limited to the waist up. Look your body up and down. *Don't* mentally edit as you go; *don't* imagine what you would look like if you were thinner or if you had a tummy-tuck or if your cellulite

magically disappeared. Take yourself in just as you are, in this very moment.

Pay attention to the feelings that come up. What are you telling yourself as you look at your body?

Please note that this exercise in particular can be very difficult for some - the emotional equivalent of battling a group of particularly ferocious demons. We are our own worst critics; when we are alone and fully present with nothing but ourselves and our naked bodies, this can leave room for the nastiest of nasty thoughts to slip in. The presence of these thoughts does *not* mean you're doing it wrong. In fact, by taking time to *just be* with yourself and your body in all its birthday-suited glory, you're doing *exactly the right thing.*

When thoughts come up, observe them impartially, the way you did in the earlier exercise in which I had you notice all the negative thoughts you had about your body throughout the day. Do your best not to form an attachment to any of them. Instead, try to come up with logical counters to each of them. I described doing this in my own bathroom: when the word "unlovable" kept coming up, for example, I would remind myself of all the people in my life who did, in fact, love me.

Do you tell your body it looks "disgusting?" Perhaps you can counter that by thinking about how often your presence in a room actually evokes reactions of real and outright *disgust* from those around you. Probably, it's not very often (and honey, if it is, please refer back to Exercise #5, because you deserve *so* much better than that).

Perhaps the feeling of "not good enough" keeps surfacing for you. Ask yourself: good enough for *what?* Because in my opinion, as long as you've got an open heart, an open mind, and a body with which to exist in, you are absolutely good enough for *anything* you should choose to take on.

Are you calling yourself a "cow?" It shouldn't take much thought at all to concede that you're very decidedly *not* actually a bovine creature with hooves and a tail, spending your days out to pasture.

Be gentle with yourself, and take your time. Do your best to deflect these thoughts, keeping your heart full and radiating feelings of love and kindness toward yourself.

If you come across a thought you can't deflect…is there any way you can own it? This was my experience with the word *fat*. I couldn't deny it - it was clear as day. Since it was a true descriptor, I shifted my focus to changing my *feelings* about the word, rather than the word *itself.* And when I owned it - when I saw it for what it was, a mere adjective and nothing more - its power to hurt me faded away.

Let's say you were tall, and not at all self-conscious about it. If someone approached you and said "You're tall," you'd shrug and reply "Yes…so?" The remark can't hurt you because you've owned it - you have no negative associations with it. Would it be possible for you to get to this place with some of the words you say to yourself in the mirror, like lumpy, lopsided, huge, or big-bellied?

I owned the word fat by saying it to myself in the mirror. "I'm fat." If you do this, be sure to state it

.

conversationally, like it's no big deal (because it really isn't). Say it like you'd say "I'm calm" or "I'm going to the store." It may help to throw in other positive, affirming phrases as well:

> "I'm fat and I'm beautiful."
> "I'm fat and I'm *gorgeous*."
> "I'm worthy, lovable, attractive, and fat."

As I mentioned before, this is a delicate practice, and it may be best done in small doses at first. If you're feeling particularly sensitive to the emotions that come up during this exercise, try to focus on either deflecting or owning just one negative thought at a time. Even one minute a day, after all, is better than zero.

The Takeaway:

We all have a narrative going on in our heads at any given time. The cool thing is, we *can* take control of that narrative, guarding it like a sentinel, either gently banishing or intentionally reframing the thoughts that cause us emotional harm. And, the more comfortable we get with being fully present to the sight of our naked bodies, the more comfortable we will be existing within those bodies.

Exercise 10:

GET REBELLIOUS

Now's the time to break all the rules.

Remember all those rules I discussed earlier? For me, some of those rules were "never reveal my legs unless I'm wearing heels" and "never wear stretchy pants unless my shirt is long enough to cover my butt." You've likely got a set of your own that you've been unconsciously allowing into your life, to govern as they see fit. It's time to ditch those rules and take back your life!

How To Do It:
First, you'll need to take stock of these rules. Make a list of anything you do, in your day to day life, that is designed to either hide, apologize for, or compensate for your body. Here are some examples to get the juices flowing:

- Eat only "good" foods, like salad, in public
- Don't show your legs/upper arms/stomach
- Don't wear anything that's too sexy
- Try to make yourself as small as possible when you're in public by pulling your arms in tightly to your sides

- Never wear a swimsuit
- Don't seek the spotlight
- Don't wear anything tight across your belly
- Never leave the house without your makeup

Et cetera, et cetera. Once you have your list, pick one rule - just one at a time - that you will commit to breaking. It's simple, but not easy.

When I broke the "don't show your legs unless you're wearing heels" rule, I felt *so* vulnerable. I emerged into the world shyly, apologetically, wishing I could put a bag over my head so no one could link me with these puffy, lumpy, straight-up-and-down legs.

But do you know what happened?

Nothing.

I'd imagined hordes of people shrinking away from the site of my pasty-white gams. Women hiding their children's faces to shield them from the horror, crowds fleeing in panic like extras in a Godzilla movie - that sort of thing. But none of that happened. Instead, people carried on about their business, with hardly a wayward glance at my legs.

Imagine that!

I feel the need to mention that - *yes* - the possibility does exist that someone will say or do something hurtful when you show up in authenticity and vulnerability. It's not a perfect world, and cruel people exist, as do those who just try to "help" by saying things that harm, humiliate, or devalue us.

But.

We can't live our lives hiding from those people. We owe it to ourselves to *be* ourselves - genuinely and authentically. And when we use our oppressive list of rules as a shield to protect ourselves from the criticisms of others... we're not really living. Not in all our fabulous, beautiful glory, anyway.

The more rules you break, the easier breaking them will become - and sooner than you think, you may be able to ditch the list entirely and live your life according to wants, desires, and loves, rather than *shoulds.*

The Takeaway:

Any rule that is informed by shame really *is* meant to be broken. And if anyone has a problem with that...it says a lot more about *them* than it does about *you.*

- 10 -
Things You Should Know

We've spent some great time together. I've shared my story, illustrated my journey, and hopefully encouraged you to embark on a journey of your own - a journey to love yourself *right now, as you are, with no strings attached.*

And here is where I leave you with some final thoughts.

No matter what you believe about yourself, or what others may believe about you based on your body, or even what others have *told* you they believe about your body, I am here to promise you that the following statements are unarguably, undeniably true.

These statements are my love notes to you. Read them as often as you need. Write the headings as affirmations on your bathroom mirror in dry-erase marker and whisper them to yourself as you get ready for your day. Reach for them if you need words of comfort, encouragement, and love. If you feel you have nothing else...you at least have these love notes.

You are strong.

How do I know this? You picked up this book, didn't you? Why did you choose it? Was it because you're tired of chasing an impossible standard and hating yourself when you cannot attain perfection? Because you want to learn more about how to overcome some of your limiting belief systems? Because you wish to treat yourself with less judgment and more love?

All of those reasons, and so many more, are centered around one thing, and that is: resisting the status quo. Picking up this book is an act of resistance - one step in the right direction - and that takes strength and courage.

Additionally, it is very difficult, in this rigidly intolerant world, to face each day under the weight of crushing insecurity about one's body. Regardless of your size, the pervasive feeling of inadequacy is a huge burden - one you've most likely been carrying around for a long time. You have to be strong as *hell* to go about your life with that huge sack of societal expectations on your back.

You also have to be strong as hell to put down the sack and continue on without this burden - and I *know* you can do it.

You are not defined by how you look.

Your body is simply a vehicle for the stuff that makes you so divinely *you*: your spirit, your heart, your passions. You could weigh five hundred pounds more than you do right now, and you would *still* be no less worthy of love and respect as a human being. Your physical frame could be five times as wide as it currently is, and it would *still* not lessen the potency of your achievements, successes, and victories. Which brings us to the next point…

You have achievements, successes, and victories.

Because so many of us who have spent our lives fully convinced of our own perceived inadequacy often have trouble tooting our own horns, I'll offer this as a reminder.

You have accomplished so much.

Here - I'll even *prove* it. Below is a list of things that are, for many of us, anywhere from slightly to extremely difficult to do - and I'm willing to bet you've done at least a few of them.

- Learned something new
- Graduated high school
- Gave a presentation
- Got a job
- Got a promotion
- Cleaned your living space
- Faced one of your fears
- Taught someone how to do something
- Graduated college
- Started at a new job or school
- Moved to a new place
- Gave birth

- Raised a child
- Saved money
- Prepared a home cooked meal
- Navigated through the ups and downs of a relationship
- Bought a house or a car
- Tried something new
- Stood up for yourself
- Made someone else feel good about themselves
- Gotten a driver's license
- Carried on with a broken heart
- Did something kind for yourself
- Apologized to someone
- Asked for help
- Got out of bed

Some of these may not seem like accomplishments to you, perhaps because you don't struggle with them. But for others, they may be formidable tasks. Even getting out of bed has, at certain points in my life, proved damn near impossible. And I'll admit to having days when getting out of bed was simply not an option. But, more often than not, when getting up and getting moving seems like a daunting task...I do it anyway. Sometimes, I do it only because I don't have a choice - because I have a job to do and responsibilities that need addressed. But regardless of the why - I *did* it. That, my friends, is an accomplishment in and of itself.

Our accomplishments deserve celebration. It doesn't matter how small they seem. If it's something that was difficult, and you got through it - put your party hat on, cupcake, because you fucking *did* it! And don't let anyone else rain on your parade just because they don't understand the particular hurdle you jumped over. Celebrate! Own your accomplishments! Toot that horn!

You're worth it.

Success, worth, and value cannot be measured by comparing yourself to someone else.

What does success look like to you? Chances are, it may look vastly different to someone else - and that's okay. Some people define success by having lots of money, or a career they're passionate about it. Others define it by raising a family, committing to a life of learning, or achieving happiness. I believe that one of the most important things you can do for yourself is to decide what success means to *you* - and *why.*

We're constantly receiving messages, both subtle and direct, about what it means to really succeed in our culture, and we tend to project these notions of success on to ourselves. Having lots of money, of course, is seen as the ultimate benchmark for success - and the drive toward riches is, I suspect, one of the main reasons why so many people don't pursue their passions, opting instead to work a high-paying job that leaves them unfulfilled and unhappy.

What else are we told we need to do or be in order to succeed? Mainstream beauty is definitely on that list. Remember my former friend who tried to convince me that Adele's weight was barring her from true success, despite the fact that at the time of our conversation, *she had already won nine Grammys?* This so clearly illustrates society's pervasive belief that, for women *especially*, real success only happens to you if you are thin and conventionally attractive. It's as though I could win forty-six Grammys, but if I did it while weighing 280 pounds, none of them would count. It's as though beauty is, in and of itself, considered a success - and that's exactly how thin and beautiful people are treated in this society. They've done something right. Their appearance is correct and in accordance with protocol. They've succeeded...except they didn't actually *do* anything, other than look the part. Sure, maybe they put in long hours at the gym - but since when are someone's personal StairMaster stats a universal success standard? Moving our bodies is a healthy and loving thing to do for ourselves, of course, but doing so is a success in and of itself - a success that has nothing to do with the way we look afterward.

What other faulty measures do we automatically use to define success? From the time we are very young, most women face societal pressure to get married and have babies. When I was a kid, no one ever asked me if I *wanted* to be a mother - they just assumed I would. As I grew older, I felt no urge toward motherhood whatsoever, and I worried about what this meant. Was there something wrong with me? I'd been raised to believe, through social conditioning, that motherhood was what was expected of me. That to succeed as a woman was to have babies and raise them into adulthood. And if I didn't want to follow that path...I worried that it would mean I had failed.

I'm now very comfortable with my decision not to birth children of my own, but it took a lot of lamenting over my "defectiveness" as a woman before I eventually made peace with it.

Not only are we given ideas of what success needs to look like, we are also told, in so many ways, that if you don't succeed, you're not worthy or valuable as a human being. In America in particular, our sense of self worth is so wrapped up in our notions of success and achievement that many of us don't even know who we are underneath all the frosting.

All these expectations floating around in the world make it very difficult to form our own ideas about what success looks like - but it's important to do it anyway. Define what success means to *you* - and make it the stuff that really matters. The stuff that will bring you soul-deep happiness and fulfillment. The stuff you will remember when your journey on Earth is coming to an end; the stuff that will make your heart swell with pride for the life you've lived. I'm willing to bet clothing size won't be on that list.

The world would be a terribly dull place if we all looked alike.

Variety is the spice of life, and diversity is brilliant and exciting and gorgeous in its authenticity. If we all suddenly looked like the most perfect specimen of mainstream beauty imaginable, we would quickly tire of that ideal and move on to something else, eventually finding ourselves feeling like shit *all over again* for not measuring up to the *new* standard.

It's a vicious cycle, and one we can't win - unless, of course, we get off the merry-go-round altogether and learn to celebrate ourselves for the unique brand of beauty that is especially, exquisitely ours and ours alone.

You are utterly, perfectly, divinely beautiful.

Right now, just as you are, in your most natural of states. Without layers to hide beneath. Without makeup or perfectly styled hair. Without disclaimers or qualifiers. Like a museum-grade masterpiece, there has never been a work of art just like you, nor will there ever be. Van Gogh, Renoir, Monet - none of them could ever recreate the likes of you. You are irreplaceable, and the world is more colorful, dimensional, and lovely because of your presence within it.

You deserve to love, to be loved, and to be happy.

You deserve these things *right now*. There is no set of conditions that has to be met first. There are no physical parameters that one must fall within in order to be worthy of love and happiness.

Your body is not a problem.

You do not need to apologize for it. You do not need to hide it. You don't have to fix it, because there's nothing wrong with it. You do not need to limit yourself and your lifestyle because of it, nor do you owe anyone an explanation for it. If someone else is bothered by some aspect of your appearance, the problem is theirs, not yours.

You can do anything you decide to do - and you can do it now.

You do not need to wait until you look a certain way, or until your body is a specific size. If you want to wear a swimsuit, you can do so whether you weigh one hundred pounds or four hundred pounds. Same applies if you want to date, or have your picture taken, or travel, or start a business, or have a child, or do yoga, or begin a new project. You are living your life right now - don't let it pass you by while you chase an unattainable standard.

I love you.

You're amazing.

You've got this.

Works Cited

1. Pai S, Schryver K. (January 2015). *Children, Teens, Media and Body Image - A Common Sense Research Brief.* Accessed November 15 2017 through https://www.commonsensemedia.org/research/children-teens-media-and-body-image.

2. Schwartz, M.B. (March 2006). The influence of one's own body weight on implicit and explicit anti-fat bias. *Obesity* 14(3): 440-447.

3. Hruschka, D. (December 2011). Shared Norms and Their Explanation for the Social Clustering of Obesity. *American Journal of Public Health* 101 Suppl 1:S295-300.

4. N. (March 2017). *The Daily Value of a Woman's Face.* Accessed November 19 2017 through http://www.skinstore.com/blog/skincare/womens-face-worth-survey-2017/.

5. Miller, K. (January 2015) *Study: Most Girls Start Dieting By Age 8.* Accessed December 12 2017 through https://www.refinery29.com/en-us/2015/01/81288/children-dieting-body-image.

6. Brown, H. (2015). *Body of Truth.* (1st edition.) 36-37. USA: DaCapo.

7. Brown, H. (2015). *Body of Truth.* (1st edition.) 59-61. USA: DaCapo.

8. Beeken R, Jackson S, Wardle J. (2014). Perceived Weight Discrimination and Changes in Weight, Waist Circumference, and Weight Status. *Obesity* 22: 2485-2488.

9. Heid, M. (January 2016). *Experts Say Lobbying Skewed the U.S. Dietary Guidelines.* Time Magazine. Accessed May 3 2018 through http://time.com/4130043/lobbying-politics-dietary-guidelines/.

10. Brown, H. (2015). *Body of Truth.* (1st edition.) 106. USA: DaCapo.

11. Flegal, K. (January 2013). Association of All-Cause Mortality With Overweight and Obesity Using Standard Body Mass Index Categories: A Systemic Review and Meta-Analysis. *Journal of the American Medical Association* 309(1):79-82.

12. Brown, H. (2015). *Body of Truth.* (1st edition.) 16-17. USA: DaCapo.

13. Heuer C, Puhl R. (2009) The Stigma of Obesity: A Review and Update. *Obesity* 17(5):941-964.

14. Friedman R, Puhl R. (2012). Weight Bias: A Social Justice Issue. Accessed March16 2018 through http://www.uconnruddcenter.org/files/Pdfs/Rudd_Policy_Brief_Weight_Bias.pdf.

15. Fruh, S. (2016). Obesity Stigma and Bias. *Journal for Nurse Practitioners* 12(7):425-432.

16. N. (May 2015). *The Economic and Societal Impact of Motor Vehicle Crashes, 2010 (Revised).* U.S. Dept of Transportation. Accessed February 6 2018 through https://crashstats.nhtsa.dot.gov/Api/Public/ViewPublication/812013.

17. N. (2016). *The Surgeon General's Report on Alcohol, Drugs, and Health.* Accessed February 6 2018 through https://www.surgeongeneral.gov/library/2016alcoholdrugshealth/index.html.

18. Xu X, Bishop EE, Kennedy SM, Simpson SA, Pechacek TF. (2014). Annual Healthcare Spending Attributable to Cigarette Smoking: An Update. *American Journal of Preventive Medicine* 48(3):326–33

19. Spitzer, SA. (May 2017). Costs and Financial Burden of Initial Hospitalizations for Firearm Injuries in the United States, 2006-2014. *American Journal of Public Health* 107(5): 770-774.
20. Wiltz, T. (November 2015). Citing Costs to Taxpayers, Cities and States Tackle Obesity. Pew Trusts. Accessed July 2 2018 through https://www.pewtrusts.org/en/research-and-analysis/blogs/stateline/2015/11/02/citing-cost-to-taxpayers-cities-and-states-tackle-obesity.
21. Wong, D. (March 2012). Five Ways Modern Men Are Trained To Hate Women: Update. Accessed October 12 2017 through http://www.cracked.com/article_19785_5-ways-modern-men-are-trained-to-hate-women.html.

About the Author

Ali Owens is a writer, speaker, self-love advocate, and empowerment strategist who is passionate about using her own experiences with healing through trauma to help empower others to do the same. She has written numerous editorials and thought pieces for several publications, including the Huffington Post and The Identity of She. As a speaker, she has traveled the country giving talks on body-positivity and unapologetic self-love and encouraging people to embrace vulnerability and speak their truths.

Ali feels most alive when she is traveling, expressing her creativity, and tapping into her intuition. She lives in the vibrant community of Fort Collins, Colorado, where she enjoys singing, sipping tea, spending time with friends, family, and pets, and seeking out new hobbies she probably doesn't have time for.

She can be found online at www.ali-owens.com.